S0-BRP-509

LAW
ENFORCEMENT
AGENCIES

INTERPOL

LAW ENFORCEMENT AGENCIES

Bomb Squad

Border Patrol

Crime Lab

Drug Enforcement Administration

Federal Bureau of Investigation

Interpol

Los Angeles Police Department

New York Police Department

The Secret Service

SWAT Teams

The Texas Rangers

U.S. Marshals

LAW
ENFORCEMENT
AGENCIES

INTERPOL

Colin Evans

CHELSEA HOUSE
An Infobase Learning Company

INTERPOL

Copyright © 2011 by Infobase Learning

All rights reserved. No part of this book may be reproduced or utilized in any form or by any means, electronic or mechanical, including photocopying, recording, or by any information storage or retrieval systems, without permission in writing from the publisher. For information contact:

Chelsea House
An imprint of Infobase Learning
132 West 31st Street
New York NY 10001

Library of Congress Cataloging-in-Publication Data

Evans, Colin, 1948-
Interpol / Colin Evans.
p. cm. — (Law enforcement agencies)
Includes bibliographical references and index.
ISBN-13: 978-1-60413-613-5 (hardcover : alk. paper)
ISBN-10: 1-60413-613-8 (hardcover : alk. paper) 1. International
Criminal Police Organization. 2. Law Enforcement—International cooperation
3. Criminal investigation—International cooperation. I. Title.
HV7240.E93 2011   363.206'01—dc22
2010048099

Chelsea House books are available at special discounts when purchased in bulk quantities for businesses, associations, institutions, or sales promotions. Please call our Special Sales Department in New York at (212) 967-8800 or (800) 322-8755.

You can find Chelsea House on the World Wide Web at http://www.infobaselearning.com

Text design and composition by Erika K. Arroyo
Cover design by Keith Trego
Cover printed by Yurchak Printing, Landisville, Penn.
Book printed and bound by Yurchak Printing, Landisville, Penn.
Date printed: April 2011

Printed in the United States of America

10 9 8 7 6 5 4 3 2 1

This book is printed on acid-free paper.

All links and Web addresses were checked and verified to be correct at the time of publication. Because of the dynamic nature of the Web, some addresses and links may have changed since publication and may no longer be valid.

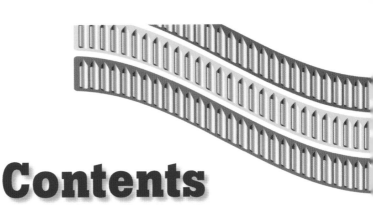

Contents

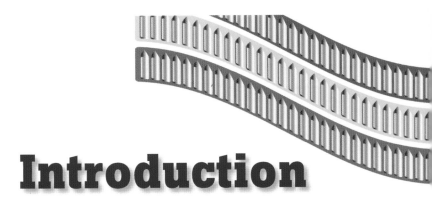

Introduction

What is an international criminal? The definition of this type of wrong-doer is not based on any legal concept—for there is no law prohibiting international crime per se—but simply on practical convenience. For example, a man who murders someone in North Carolina and then flees to Mexico can be classified as an international criminal. So, too, is the con man who travels from country to country, able to ply his trade at every stopping-off point. But what are law enforcement officials to make of the British counterfeiter, for example, who daily prints thousands of illegal $100 bills? He may never travel farther afield than the London suburb where his illegal printing press is based, yet he too must be considered an international criminal. This is because, within days, his forgeries could be circulating as far away as Japan or Australia. Try telling the person left holding fistfuls of worthless currency that he or she has not been a victim of international crime!

The fight against the international criminal began in the last days of the Victorian age (1837–1901). This was an era packed with advances in the field of forensic science—so many, in fact, that some law enforcement officers were predicting the virtual extinction of the criminal class. In 1906 Sir Henry Smith, commissioner of police for the city of London, encapsulated this arrogance when he sounded almost pitying as he lamented the hapless lawbreaker's " . . . want of originality [and] strange stupidity."[1] Such fools, it was thought, would be hopelessly outgunned by the advent of fingerprinting, blood grouping, and other miracles of the crime lab. Unfortunately, Smith overlooked one critical phenomenon: the development of mass transport.

Whereas the Victorian criminal had to make do with foot- or horse-power, his 20th-century counterpart could call on the automobile and the train to whisk him across international frontiers. It had never been

The Interpol logo is displayed on the floor of the agency's headquarters in Lyon, France. *(AP Photo/Laurent Cipriani)*

easier—or quicker—for the ambitious criminal to widen his theater of operations. It was against this backdrop that Interpol was formed.

Before going any further, an important clarification is required: Interpol is *not* a police force. Despite what some TV programs and movies would have one believe, there are no Interpol detectives busting down doors and arresting criminals from far-off lands. Interpol has no powers of arrest, search, or seizure. All it can do is advise. Any further action relies entirely on the law enforcement agencies of its 188 member countries. It is best to think of Interpol as a vast international clearinghouse of crime and criminal data. Information pours in around the clock to Interpol's headquarters in Lyon, France, where it is handled by a staff that is constantly changing. One-third of staff members are temporary, drawn from the police forces of its member nations for a set period of time (the remainder are permanent civil servants). Once their tour of duty is over—two years is a typical assignment—these police officers return to their home countries and replacements come in from other countries. This temporary staffing is done on a strict

THE NOTICES

At the heart of Interpol's information-disseminating machine is its legendary "Notice" program. There are now seven categories of notice, each prioritized and color-coded accordingly. Once a notice has been compiled it is then circulated to member nations. Generally speaking, the notice contains two main types of information. First, there is a comprehensive description of the wanted person. This will include identity details such as a comprehensive physical description, photograph, fingerprints where possible, and other relevant information such as occupation, any languages spoken, and the numbers of known identity documents such as passports and visas. The second part of the notice deals with judicial information. In most cases it will list the offense with which the person is charged; explain the laws under which the charge has been made; and lay out the maximum penalty that can be imposed. This is critical, because it will generally include references to any possible legal ramifications. For instance, if a fugitive from a justice system that employs capital punishment is apprehended in a country that does not have the death penalty, then there is likely to be a lengthy sparring session over extradition. The notice prepares both countries for this outcome.

Notices are posted in English, Arabic, French and Spanish (the organization's official working languages). All notices are published on Interpol's secure Web site, which can only be accessed by authorized law enforcement agencies. However, if the requesting country agrees, some notices are also published on the organization's public Web site. This is in recognition of the vital part played by the general public when it comes to arresting international criminals. The following is a list of the various Interpol notices:

★ **Red Notice:** So called from the red-flagged corner, this is the highest priority of all. It seeks the apprehension of a wanted

(continues)

(continued)

person based on an arrest warrant or court decision. Most member countries regard a Red Notice as a valid request for provisional arrest.

★ **Blue Notice:** This is a request for additional information about a person's identity, location, or illegal activities in relation to a criminal matter.

★ **Green Notice:** These notices provide warnings or criminal intelligence about persons who have committed criminal offenses and are likely to repeat these crimes in other countries.

★ **Yellow Notice:** This and the Black Notice, unlike the others, usually do not deal with criminals. The Yellow Notice is a request to help locate missing persons, especially minors, or to help identify persons, such as amnesiacs, who are not able to identify themselves.

★ **Black Notice:** These notices request information about unidentified bodies.

★ **Orange Notice:** Interpol issues Orange Notices to warn police, public entities, and other international organizations of dangerous materials, criminal acts, or events that pose a potential threat to public safety.

★ **Interpol–United Nations Security Council Special Notice:** Introduced in 2005, this is a highly specific notice and is designed to alert law enforcement agencies about groups and individuals who are the target of UN sanctions against Al-Qaeda and the Taliban.

Some indication of the way in which serious international crime has exploded in recent years can be gauged from Interpol data. In 2007, for the first time in its history, Interpol issued more than 3,000 red notices in a single year, almost triple the number requested by member countries in 2000, and more than all other notices combined.

rotational basis that is designed to afford equal representation to every member nation. (Political sensibilities are never far beneath the surface at Interpol, where senior officials strive constantly to maintain a balance between expedience and equilibrium.) While serving their time at

FOFANA Youssouf   N° DE CONTROLE : B-68/2-2006

PAYS DEMANDEUR : FRANCE
N° DE DOSSIER : 2006/9335
DATE D'EDITION : 21 février 2006

1.   ELEMENTS D'IDENTIFICATION

BLEUE

1.1   NOM DE FAMILLE ACTUEL : FOFANA
1.2   NOM DE FAMILLE A LA NAISSANCE : Non précisé
1.3   PRENOM(S) : Youssouf   1.4   SEXE : M
1.5   DATE ET LIEU DE NAISSANCE : 2 août 1980 - Paris (France)
1.6   AUTRE(S) NOM(S) : Non précisé
1.7   AUTRE(S) DATE(S) DE NAISSANCE : Non précisé
1.8   NOM DE FAMILLE ET PRENOM(S) DU PERE : FOFANA Bakari
1.9   NOM DE JEUNE FILLE ET PRENOM(S) DE LA MERE : KONE Fatouma
1.10   IDENTITE INCERTAINE
1.11   NATIONALITE FRANCAISE (EXACTE)
1.12   PIECE(S) D'IDENTITE : Non précisé
1.13   PROFESSION : Non précisé
1.14   LANGUE(S) PARLEE(S) : Français
1.15   SIGNALEMENT : Non précisé
1.16   MARQUES PARTICULIERES ET CARACTERISTIQUES : Non précisé
1.17   CODE ADN : Non précisé
1.18   REGION(S) / PAYS OU L'INDIVIDU EST SUSCEPTIBLE DE SE RENDRE : Burkina Faso, Bénin,
        Côte D'Ivoire, Ghana, Guinée, Libéria, Maroc, Mali, Niger, Sénégal, Togo
1.19   RENSEIGNEMENTS COMPLEMENTAIRES : Non précisé

2.   ELEMENTS RELATIFS A L'ENQUETE CRIMINELLE

2.1   EXPOSE DES FAITS :

        FRANCE :

        FOFANA est suspecté d'être l'instigateur de l'enlèvement et l'auteur présumé de l'assassinat commis au
        préjudice du dénommé Ilan HALIMI dans la nuit du 20 au 21 janvier 2006. La victime est décédée des
        suites de ses blessures le 13 février 2006. Son corps a été découvert à Sainte Geneviève des bois,
        Essonne.

An Interpol Blue Notice identifies Youssouf Fofana, wanted for kidnapping and murder. Interpol uses its seven color-coded notices to disseminate information to law enforcement agencies, and sometimes civilians, around the world. *(AFP/Getty Images)*

Lyon, these officers assess the information received and prioritize it for future action. There are seven levels of seriousness and each of these is given a color-coded notice. These notices are then circulated around the globe within seconds. In this way, member nations can be kept up to date on wanted fugitives, the latest scams, and cutting-edge developments in crime fighting.

COMPUTER CRIME

Constant vigilance is necessary because, in this day and age, crime is truly global. And nothing has rendered borders more meaningless than the personal computer. With a mouse click somewhere in Africa or Asia, a bank account holder in Brooklyn could suddenly see his or her net worth plunge by thousands of dollars. Ironically, although computers and modern telecommunications are a boon to the international cybercriminal, they also make Interpol's job that much easier. In 1935 Interpol made a groundbreaking advance in law enforcement when it launched its own dedicated radio network. At the time, this was state-of-the-art technology. Nowadays, mainframe computers and lightning-fast telecommunications mean that Interpol, as it continues the never-ending battle against international crime, can keep in instant touch with the whole world.

TERRORISM

All law enforcement agencies are subject to the whims of their political masters, but Interpol is truly unique in that no other crime fighting organization has to balance the needs and demands of 188 different governments. It is a monumental task, and there have been times when Interpol has struggled with the challenge. Nowhere has this been more apparent than in the organization's response to international terrorism. For instance, when members of the Black September Organization, a Palestinian militant group, broke into the Olympic Village in Munich in 1972 and massacred 11 Israeli athletes and coaches, Interpol flatly refused to become involved in a wider search for other terrorists who might have been involved. Interpol's excuse was that its charter prohibited it from involvement in any investigation deemed to have political overtones, but the real reasons went much deeper than that. The fact was that much of the money that funded Black September, and groups like it, came from the governments of countries who were members of Interpol, and these nations were in no hurry to see their divided loyalties made public. It took several years and several more atrocities before Interpol finally recognized terrorism for what it is: an international crime against the whole world. Interpol is now thoroughly integrated into the war on terror and assists in hunting down fugitives, regardless of their country of origin.

Crime never stands still, and the criminal is always looking for a way to gain an edge. It might be a key-logger Trojan, designed to infect

PASSPORT CONTROL

In the early days of the 20th century the pickings were rich for the swindler. A slick con man could hit a jeweler's store in Paris and—barely a day later—be dining out on the proceeds of that heist in a Venetian restaurant. Along the way he could cross most international borders in Europe without showing identification papers of any kind. All that changed after the First World War. Suddenly nations became far more protective of their borders. In October 1920 the International Conference on Passports was held in Paris under the auspices of the League of Nations (a precursor to the United Nations), and a model form of passport—opening like a book, containing a fixed number of pages, certain items of personal description, and a photograph of the holder—was adopted by most member states. Such an innovation made it much easier to keep tabs on people, especially criminals. However, agreement was one thing, and implementation another. It took another decade of squabbling and tweaking before the model passport became a reality. On March 27, 1932, over the Easter weekend, a majority of Interpol member states formally adopted an internationally recognized standard passport. At long last, the police forces of the world had a new weapon with which to fight the increasingly flagrant international trickster.

computers worldwide and thereby potentially gain access to millions of bank accounts, or it could be a handful of fanatics holed up in a Afghanistan cave, plotting to wreak havoc on a civil population half a world away. Where once most crime was local—pickpocketing, burglary, and assault, for example—now it can be remote, with criminal and victim separated by several time zones and even continents. Although the founders of Interpol, in the early 20th century, could never have dreamt of such developments, they recognized that crime was changing; and that same realization is very much alive today, only more so.

Interpol examines the history, techniques, successes, and shortcomings of the global crime-fighting organization. The book consists of seven chapters.

Chapter 1, "A Noble Idea," outlines the origins of Interpol and how it evolved after World War 1.

Chapter 2, "A Murder in the Woods," demonstrates the coordinated action of various international policing organizations in the chaos that emerged after World War II.

Chapter 3, "The Phantom Shipment," reveals the scale and scope of international fraud through the machinations of one of the 20th century's most devious tricksters.

Chapter 4, "Washing the Money," provides an in-depth look at how Interpol helped bring down one of the biggest drug-trafficking rings in the United States.

Chapter 5, "The Boiler Room," deals with so-called white-collar crime and a share-dealing scam that cheated investors out of millions.

Chapter 6, "The Long-Distance Killer," delves into the way Interpol pursued a serial killer who murdered victims in Austria, Czechoslovakia, and Los Angeles.

Chapter 7, "Unmasking 'Mr. Swirl,'" provides insight into how Interpol is at the forefront of the fight against child sexual abuse, helping to track down offenders who operate globally.

A Noble Idea

The idea for an international, coordinated approach to crime fighting had an unlikely birthplace. Monaco, a sun-drenched outcrop perched on the southern coastline of France, is one of the world's smallest countries, barely a mile square in area. It is famed as a playground for the mega-rich and the glamorous. They come for the low taxes, the world-renowned casino, the glorious year-round weather, and simply to be seen. Crime is virtually unknown. And yet it was here, in the spring of 1914, that delegates from 24 countries gathered to lay the foundations for the organization now called Interpol. They came at the request of Prince Albert I of Monaco. Like his country, he seemed an improbable host for such an event. There were rumors—nothing more—that Albert's sudden interest was born out of a deep humiliation. Monaco gossip hinted that the ruler had recently fallen for the charms of a young beauty, only to find that while he and his paramour had been playing the casino's tables, the young woman's lover had ransacked the prince's private quarters in the palace and made off with jewelry and other valuables. The thief had then crossed the border into Italy—and safety—just 10 miles away. Albert was reportedly so incensed by this international immunity that he decided something needed to be done. This meeting was the outcome.

The congress began on April 14, 1914, under the presidency of the dean of the law faculty of the University of Paris. Delegates came not only from Europe but also from Brazil, Cuba, Guatemala, and even as far away as Asia. Most of the world's major police forces were represented, but not every nation was convinced. Britain, confident that Scotland Yard needed no assistance, merely sent along a handful of low-ranking lawyers to observe the proceedings. The United States, even more skeptical, made do with a solitary judge from Dayton, Ohio. However, what the attendees heard was impressive. The delegates passed important resolutions calling for the establishment of a centralized system of international criminal records, as well as plans for the first standardized, speedy extradition procedure, that would operate in every country in the world. Then came some procedural decisions. It was decided that French would be the common language and that a second congress would be held in August 1916 in Bucharest, the capital of Romania. On April 20 the delegates began returning to their respective countries, bursting with enthusiasm.

Three months later the dream was dead. On June 28, in the broiling streets of Sarajevo, an assassin's gun shot Archduke Franz Ferdinand of Austro-Hungary and his wife, killing them both. Within weeks the world was at war. Soon, all plans for the establishment of a coordinated crime-fighting organization were buried beneath the mud of the Western Front (a term used in World War I and World War II to describe the contested area between lands held by Germany to the east and the Allies to the west).

When Europe emerged from the horrors of the First World War in 1918, it was a shattered continent. As always, criminals thrived in the chaos. Black market "entrepreneurs" pocketed fortunes by taking advantage of recently redrawn national borders that made it all too easy to shift goods and people across frontiers. Austria was a country affected more than most by this upsurge in crime. The war had taken a terrible toll on the once proud nation. It had shrunk to a fraction of its former size geographically and its political impact was now virtually negligible. One man vowed to restore some semblance of national pride. Johann Schober might have been the chancellor of Austria, but his background was in law enforcement, and in May 1922 he resigned the chancellorship to return to his former job as president of the state police force. One of his dreams was to resurrect Prince Albert's idea of an international police organization, but this time it would be based in Vienna. He sent out over 300 invitations to police chiefs around the world to attend a "Second International Criminal Police Congress" at the Austrian capital in September 1923.

He got a mixed response. Of the 138 delegates who assembled in Vienna on Monday, September 3, only 67 came from abroad; the rest were homegrown (to spare Schober's pride, they had been drafted in). Even so, 17 countries were represented and most came from western Europe,

Austrian politician and lawman Johann Schober was Interpol's first president. *(Hulton Archive/Getty Images)*

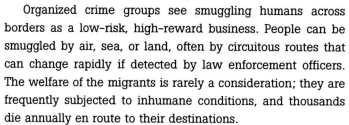

CATCHING THE PEOPLE SMUGGLERS

The desire to improve one's lot in life is genetically hardwired. When modern humans first left Africa, they went in search of places that would improve their way of life. Nothing has changed. One hundred thousand years later, millions of people around the globe cast envious eyes at some foreign land and think, "I wish I could live there." But the days of easy migration are over. In the 19th century millions of hopeful immigrants flooded into America each year. Now they have to battle a strict quota system. It is the same in most developed countries. However, no amount of legislation will stop the dream, and it will not stop criminals from exploiting that dream.

Illegal migration and people smuggling are not new phenomena, but the last two decades have seen dramatic changes in the scale of the problem. All around the world there are gangs prepared to smuggle people illegally across international borders. The type of operation varies enormously from one country to another, but Interpol's focus is on the highly organized networks that reap huge profits from this trade.

Organized crime groups see smuggling humans across borders as a low-risk, high-reward business. People can be smuggled by air, sea, or land, often by circuitous routes that can change rapidly if detected by law enforcement officers. The welfare of the migrants is rarely a consideration; they are frequently subjected to inhumane conditions, and thousands die annually en route to their destinations.

Most will have paid in advance, although some gangs accept a down payment, with the balance due either from relatives in the home country or else from the migrants them-

although this time the United States did attend in force. On September 7, 1923, a brand new phenomenon in world policing came into being—the International Criminal Police Commission (ICPC). Its role was laid out in the following terms: "To establish and develop all institutions likely to contribute to the efficient suppression of ordinary law crime."[1]

selves shortly after arrival. Those unable to pay anything often find themselves steered into the clutches of loan sharks with close connections to the smuggler. As soon as payment for the smuggling operation is completed, the relationship between the illegal immigrant and the smuggler is generally terminated. This is where Interpol draws a distinction between people smuggling and human trafficking. In the latter case, migrants are exploited upon arrival in another country, usually for forced labor or prostitution. They endure a horrible existence.

Each year Interpol adds to its databases of criminal networks that deal in people smuggling, and it has isolated certain regions as being especially problematic. Currently it is West Africa that is under heightened scrutiny. Certain countries in that region are known to be transit states for huge outflows of migrants. They come not just from Africa but also from as far afield as Afghanistan, India, and Bangladesh. Many have already traveled thousands of miles on their journey to either Europe or North America. When news of a suspected people-smuggling incident reaches Interpol headquarters, it can issue what is called an HST (Human Smuggling and Trafficking) message. This has standardized the format for reporting such incidents and informs the member states of the latest developments. At the same time, Interpol provides operational assistance by making its databases directly accessible to border and immigration authorities around the globe.

Cooperation is key. In order to achieve its aims, Interpol works closely with several other international organizations, including the United Nations Office on Drugs and Crime.

It was an Austrian-run operation from top to bottom. Schober, of course, was elected president; the staff was entirely Austrian; the facilities were donated by the Vienna city police department; the Austrian police files formed the nucleus of what would become a new international criminal records office; and for the first five years every penny spent on the new commission's work came from the Austrian government. Only at the 1928 General Assembly did the member states finally agree to an independent funding scheme that was based on a country's population—one Swiss franc for every 10,000 inhabitants.

AMERICAN DOUBTS

Strangely, there were doubts as to which countries had actually joined the new organization. For instance, although the United States had attended the 1923 congress, it was still reluctant to commit itself to something that resembled an Austrian-run gentleman's club. When J. Edgar Hoover was appointed director of the Federal Bureau of Investigation (FBI) in 1924, this skepticism only hardened. (Hoover's attitude—one of "wait and see"—would remain the default American stance toward the ICPC until 1938, when the FBI finally yielded to the forces of history and joined.)

An important development came at the 1925 General Assembly, held in Berlin, when it was decided that each member nation should establish a central point of contact within its police structure. This was the forerunner of the National Central Bureau (NCB) system that was later adopted throughout the organization.

In 1930, at the sixth meeting, the ICPC agreed that in the future the commission would select its president and vice presidents at meetings of the General Assembly by a majority vote. The periods of office were laid down as five years for the president and two for vice presidents.

Slowly the ICPC began to flex its muscle. The General Secretariat (administrative body), with permanent departments independent of Vienna, gradually came into being, in accordance with the alterations in the statute. The departments provided five distinct services for its members.

1. The Central International Bureau for the suppression of counterfeiting banknotes, checks and other valuable securities
2. The monthly periodical entitled *International Public Security*, an informative booklet written in French and English
3. The International Criminal Records Office
4. A service dealing with the fingerprints and photographs of international criminals
5. The Central Bureau for the suppression of passport forgery

Establishment of the General Secretariat did mark the first gentle loosening of the ties with Austria. Those bonds, however, were retightened just two years later, in 1932, following the death of Schober. It was decided that, henceforth, the new chief of the ICPC would be called Secretary General, and the first person appointed to this post was yet another Austrian, Oskar Dressler.

It was Dressler who oversaw the introduction of an international radio network specifically dedicated to the needs of the ICPC. For the first time, law enforcement communities on every continent could speak to each other, safe in the knowledge that their conversations were not being tapped.

More than the radio network, it was the events in neighboring Germany that really sent tremors through the ICPC and its member nations. Adolf Hitler's rise to power in 1933 had triggered a dangerous shift in German representation at the various congresses. Where once the German delegates had been professional policemen, now they were hardened, aggressive Nazis. Kurt Daluege, who attended the Copenhagen General Assembly in 1935, typified this trend. At the time he was chief of the German police and, when asked how he had managed to progress so far so fast, boasted, "My chief qualification is that I have been in almost every cell in the Moabit Prison in Berlin."[2] Other German delegates during the 1930s included the police commissioner for Berlin, Count Graf von Helldorf, a savage anti-Semite who had gained his promotion to senior rank because of his efficiency in burning down and desecrating Jewish synagogues. Another was Arthur Nebe, the only Nazi ICPC delegate with a genuine background in police work, having been a detective in Berlin since 1920. Germany did not just attempt to seize control of the ICPC; it was now the major power in Europe and ready to flex its military might.

On March 12, 1938, Hitler's army marched into Austria. Overnight, the country virtually ceased to exist, swallowed up by the Nazi empire. As a direct result of this invasion, Germany's most powerful policeman, Heinrich Himmler, now became chief of police in Austria as well, and his second-in-command, Reinhard Heydrich, was desperate to grasp direct control of the International Criminal Police Commission. At that year's ICPC General Assembly, held in Bucharest, the Nazi caucus maneuvered to take outright control of the commission. With every delegate present realizing that war was imminent, it was accordingly proposed that the headquarters be moved away from Vienna to some

CRIME 24/7

As national boundaries become increasingly meaningless to criminals, effective police communication across borders is more important than ever before. This is where Interpol comes in. Its primary function is to enable the world's police to exchange information securely and rapidly. This was the motivation in 2002 that led Interpol to establish I-24/7, a global police communications system designed to connect law enforcement officers in its member countries, enabling authorized users to share crucial police data with one another and to access the organization's databases and services 24 hours a day.

The I-24/7 network enables investigators to make connections between seemingly unrelated pieces of information, thereby facilitating investigations and helping solve crimes. Authorized users can search and cross-check data in a matter of seconds, with direct access to databases on suspected criminals or wanted persons, stolen and lost travel documents, stolen motor vehicles and their documentation, fingerprints, DNA profiles, and stolen works of art.

In January 2003 Canada became the first country to connect to I-24/7. By 2008 all member countries were connected, and limited access had also been granted to other international organizations. Solutions have been developed to ensure that all member countries can access the system regardless of financial or technical limitations, including connection by satellite. While I-24/7 is installed at all Interpol National Crime Bureaus, many member countries have chosen to extend access to other national law enforcement entities at strategic locations, such as border crossings, airports, and customs and immigration posts.

neutral country. Switzerland was the favored option. After a tense debate, with plenty of behind-the-scenes arm-twisting by the Nazis, this suggestion was rejected by the General Assembly. Despite what was seen as only a temporary blip, the congress broke up amicably, intending to reconvene the following year in Berlin. But history overtook them. In September 1939 the world was once again at war.

NAZI TAKEOVER

This was Heydrich's golden opportunity. In early 1940 he laid down a formal proposal that the general headquarters be transferred from Vienna to Berlin, and he gave member countries just three weeks to respond. At the end of that time, delegates who had not answered were deemed to have expressed a tacit agreement. Just as Heydrich thought, few bothered to reply. As a consequence, in 1941 all the ICPC records were shipped to Berlin, and Heydrich, courtesy of a rigged election, installed himself as president. (Dressler, although still officially secretary general, blended discreetly into the background.)

With Europe under a Nazi siege, the ICPC became little more than an arm of the Gestapo, Germany's state police. Idealism was tossed out the door and for the remainder of the war all attempts at international cooperation between police forces were doomed. Other countries, most notably Britain and France, dismayed by such flagrant international muscle flexing, withdrew their support and the ICPC lapsed into impotence.

Heydrich was a man of extraordinary cruelty and ambition. It was this violin-playing psychopath who in January 1942 hosted a conference in a Berlin suburb at which he and other leading Nazis discussed "the final solution to the Jewish question." The deliberately ambiguous language was merely a smokescreen, designed to mask a blueprint for the deportation and murder of Europe's Jews. Over cognac and cigars, Heydrich and his henchmen hatched plans that would slaughter millions.

But Heydrich would never live to see his plan put into practice. Four months later, on May 27, while he was driving through Prague, Czechoslovakia, his car came under fire from two British-trained agents. Although wounded, at first Heydrich did not seem severely injured, but one week later he succumbed to septicemia (invasion of the bloodstream by virulent microorganisms and bacteria along with toxins from a local infection). The presidency of the ICPC now passed into the hands of

From 1940 to 1942, German SS General Reinhard Heydrich served as president of Interpol. Between 1938 and 1945, various SS generals chaired the organization. *(AP Photo)*

Police officers sort and route information in the command and coordination room of Interpol. *(AFP/Getty Images)*

two other Germans; first, Arthur Nebe, and then, in 1943, Ernst Kaltenbrunner. (Ironically, both ended their days at the end of a hangman's noose: Nebe for complicity in the July 20, 1944, plot to assassinate Hitler; Kaltenbrunner, in 1946, for war crimes.)

When hostilities ceased in May 1945, a new kind of war erupted across Europe, as a crime wave swept through the continent. It was imperative that nations resurrect the ICPC as soon as possible. With Dressler discreetly ousted as secretary general—his tolerance of the Nazis was unacceptable—and Austria now an occupied country, it was decided to move the headquarters to Paris, and in 1946 the organization was reborn. Louis Ducloux of France was named secretary-general.

The ICPC's most urgent problem was trying to reestablish its criminal record database. All the records made before 1938 had been shipped to Germany. Fortunately, the Belgian police had managed to keep most of its records intact and some were also eventually recovered from the bombed ruins in Berlin. It was during this period that the organization first became known as Interpol. When Ducloux retired in 1951, he handed over the reins of power to his fellow Frenchman Marcel Sicot.

One last name change came in 1956, when it was decided that the organization's full title should read International Criminal Police Organization (it was thought to sound more official). But by this time, in the mind of the public, it was known as Interpol.

As the scope and importance of Interpol grew, so did its staff. When Sicot took over he inherited 40 detectives and offices that had moved to the French Ministry of the Interior on Boulevard Gouvion St. Cyr, Paris. There they remained until moving in 1989 to the present location, at 200 Quai Charles de Gaulle, in France's "second city," Lyon.

Interpol's reach now spans the entire globe. There are currently 188 member nations (Samoa was the last to join, on October 22, 2009), all able to exchange sensitive material on a secure communications network. Interpol endures a punishing workload. In 2007 no fewer than 10 million messages were exchanged between the General Secretariat in Lyon and the National Central Bureaus in each country. The business of catching international criminals has never been easy. Without Interpol, it would be impossible.

A Murder in the Woods

The Second World War might have dealt a grievous blow to the notion of international policing, but it had utterly destroyed Berlin. In 1945 the city was a crumbled ruin. And the chaos that enveloped Hitler's capital as his "Thousand Year Reich" collapsed would form the backdrop to one of the strangest cases that the ICPC ever investigated.

In the fall of 1945 two German ex-soldiers, Manfred Schroder and Robert Laub, trudged wearily across the battle-scarred wasteland of western Poland. Their clothes were in rags, their boots badly worn, and they were exhausted, but they counted themselves fortunate. For the past four years they had fought on most of the battlefronts of Europe, but that had been a picnic compared to the last six months, which they had spent in a Soviet prisoner-of-war camp at Sagan (what is now Żagań), in Poland. Many German soldiers captured by the Russian army were simply shot or else transported to labor camps in the Soviet Union. But not Schroder and Laub. Somehow they managed to negotiate their release. Along with thousands of other refugees in that year, they began walking west, determined to reach the Allied Zone. Fifty foot-blistering miles brought them to the shattered city of Cottbus, near the recently redrawn Polish border. Another 70 miles would see them to their destination, Berlin. At Cottbus railroad station, Schroder and Laub joined hundreds of other refugees thronging the platform. Everyone, it seemed, had but one goal—escaping to the west. Fighting their way through the crowds, they eventually found space aboard a freight train bound for the capital.

It was after midnight when their train wheezed into Berlin's main rail station. The devastation that greeted them was appalling. One of Europe's architectural gems had been reduced to a blackened shell by relentless Allied bombing. Schroder, tall and thin, stumbled his way disbelievingly through the debris. Laub, with his short legs and wheezy breathing, panted as he tried to keep pace with his more athletic companion. It had been more than a year since Schroder had last seen his wife, Olga. Now, when he reached their former home, it was nothing but rubble. Like thousands of other Berliners, Olga had simply vanished. Inquiries at the town hall as to her fate were met with shrugs.

Schroder was far from overwhelmed by grief. A pragmatist down to his patched boots, just days later he was living with a prostitute named Dorle, who installed Laub in the apartment of her friend Lotte Klinger. Klinger fell heavily for Laub. She was ready to give up the streets and wanted to marry him. She was even prepared to sell her modern apartment and furniture. With the 20,000 marks ($2,000) that would bring, she reckoned they had enough to set up a permanent home.

Schroder immediately sensed an opportunity. He knew that Laub did not really care about getting married, but 20,000 marks in postwar Berlin was a king's ransom. He and Laub hatched a plan. They waited until October 3, 1945, when Klinger had realized her assets, then all three took the train out to Wannsee, southwest of Berlin. The stated intent was to travel on to Potsdam, but with a scheduled five-hour delay between trains, they left their baggage at Wannsee train station and began exploring the nearby woods and shimmering lakes. (Ironically, it was in this very oasis of tranquility, on January 20, 1942, that Heydrich chaired the infamous Wannsee Conference, in which he outlined the "final solution to the Jewish question.")

After half an hour spent trudging along paths covered with pine needles, Schroder grumbled that he was tired and needed a rest. His companions joined him as he settled down on the soft moss. Klinger soon fell fast asleep. Laub motioned to Schroder, who slunk off into the woods. When he returned his fist was clamped around an iron bar.

Silently he crept up behind Klinger and swung the bar down on her head with crushing force. Her single scream was cut off by Laub clamping his hand over her mouth. Another blow and she slumped, lifeless. The two killers wasted no time. They rifled through Klinger's belongings, then buried her in a shallow grave. After this, they hiked back to the train station, reclaimed their baggage, and returned to Berlin, eager to spend all that money.

Their fun did not last long. Just days later, word filtered through the underworld grapevine that the police were looking for Klinger. Immediately the two men fled to Saxony (a state in Germany) and a village where Laub had once worked on a farm. He changed his name to Werbl, while Schroder took the name of a married aunt called Pilger. Within weeks they were on the move again. By this time Schroder had met a young woman named Marika, and she joined the fugitives as they headed for Sternbach, some 10 miles away. Laub had a sister who lived here, and she agreed to house the trio. During this stopover, Schroder married Marika.

Then it was business as usual, with both men dealing in the black market. Schroder's unpredictable temper made him difficult to be around, however, and Laub's sister showed him the door. In January 1946 Schroder and Marika took off, leaving Laub to fend for himself. Without the crafty Schroder around to oversee operations, Laub began taking risks. Some months later he was stopped by two police officers near the Czechoslovakia border. In his rucksack they found contraband sugar, pens, and ammunition. He was arrested under his false name, but before long his true identity was revealed, as was his relationship to Lotte Klinger.

Laub's sister, setting aside any personal grievances, warned Schroder of her brother's arrest. He told Marika to get ready; they were leaving immediately. When Marika balked, Schroder knocked her unconscious, tied her up, and bolted off alone in a stolen car. He drove south toward Austria. Once across the border he would be safe. Or so he thought.

What Schroder did not know was that, in the summer of 1946, the concept of international policing had been revived. In June of that year the ICPC had a new secretary-general, a new headquarters in Paris, and

REKINDLING THE FLAME

Europe was in chaos when World War II ended. The whole continent had become a paradise for the international crook and the black market "merchant." Interpol, too, was in sorry shape. All of its records had been taken by the Nazis, destroying two decades of diligence. If the organization was ever going to regain its former status, something radical needed to be done, and quickly. The first step on this path to recovery came in Brussels, on June 3, 1946, when delegates from 17 countries attended a special conference. The United States was a notable absentee (Hoover's prewar suspicion of Interpol had resurfaced). At this conference, references to Dressler were swept under the carpet as embarrassing details of his wartime coziness with the Nazis began to emerge. As a result Dressler found himself shepherded off into a discreet retirement. His replacement as secretary general was Louis Ducloux, the widely respected former head of the French Criminal Investigation Department. During the occupation of France, Ducloux had been relieved of his duties by the Nazis, and it was clear that he was not sympathetic to the Nazis (as Dressler and others had demonstrated, not everyone in the Interpol hierarchy could make this claim). Also at this conference, delegates came up with a new funding structure for Interpol, based on a levy of 2.5 Swiss francs per 10,000 inhabitants for nations with a population of fewer than 10 million; larger states paid proportionally more.

The most contentious issue under discussion was what to do about Interpol's headquarters. Austria's close links with

a new name, Interpol (although its full title remained the International Criminal Police Commission). It also had a revived determination to pursue criminals across international borders, and one of the criminals that Interpol wanted most was Manfred Schroder.

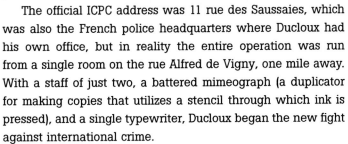

wartime Germany had destroyed Vienna's credibility, and delegates eager to draw a curtain over the past began casting around for a new location. Two countries—the Netherlands and Czechoslovakia—lobbied hard for the prize. For different reasons, neither The Hague nor Prague appealed as an option. Some delegates were put off by the blatant Dutch electioneering, while others feared that Prague would merely be a tool of Moscow, as the Soviet Union's influence was already beginning to make itself felt in Eastern Europe. Then someone mentioned Ducloux. His reputation was impeccable; why not shift Interpol's headquarters to his home city of Paris? In the absence of any objection, Paris was chosen, beginning a close association between Interpol and France that endures to the present day.

The official ICPC address was 11 rue des Saussaies, which was also the French police headquarters where Ducloux had his own office, but in reality the entire operation was run from a single room on the rue Alfred de Vigny, one mile away. With a staff of just two, a battered mimeograph (a duplicator for making copies that utilizes a stencil through which ink is pressed), and a single typewriter, Ducloux began the new fight against international crime.

And it was there, on July 22, 1946, that history was made. On that day, Jean Népote, who for all intents and purposes ran the ICPC until his retirement in 1978, called the post office and registered the name INTERPOL—a contraction of "international police"—as the organization's telegraphic address. No one had any idea just how famous that name would become.

HIDEOUT IN AUSTRIA

Schroder, unaware of this renewed interest in his whereabouts, had taken refuge in the village of Lerchenau, 20 miles north of Vienna. With his sister Carlotta living close by and helping him at every turn, Schroder dropped off the official radar. Then fate played a hand. One day, while leaving the mill where he worked, he narrowly avoided running down two police officers. It was unintended, but when Schroder returned later that day, the officers were waiting for him and they had used the hiatus to run some background checks. They told him he was wanted for questioning in connection with the Berlin murder. Schroder's slick tongue moved into action. He protested his ignorance of any murder. He said he had stayed one month in Berlin, before moving to Vienna in October 1946. If there had been a murder, then obviously that rat Laub had committed it and was trying to implicate his old friend. The police, unconvinced by Schroder's protestations, threw him into Eisenburg prison.

Laub, meanwhile, dictated a formal statement, claiming that Schroder had taken Klinger into the forest alone, killed her, and then forced him to help with the burial. At the Eisenburg prison, Schroder made a similar statement blaming Laub. In February 1947 Laub was sentenced to death, but the court stayed his execution until Schroder could be brought to trial. Poor postwar communications meant there was a delay in conveying this news to the Austrian authorities.

Schroder was already planning his escape. Although his barred cell window was set high up, he knew that it overlooked the 25-foot-high prison wall. Beyond this lay the open road. After some thought, he contacted Carlotta. Acting on Schroder's orders, she baked a cake and topped it off with a small figurine. Attached to this, and secreted inside the cake, was a tiny ball of fine twine. On her next visit, Carlotta succeeded in smuggling the cake to Schroder. That night at around 10:00 P.M., he dropped the weighted twine down from his window. Carlotta, waiting outside the prison wall, quickly attached a tiny handsaw to the twine and watched as it was drawn up. Over the next days and nights Schroder carefully sawed almost through the bars on his cell window. Finally, on the morning of March 20, the work was completed. All that was now required was a slight push.

At just after midnight, Schroder and his cellmate pushed out the bars and climbed onto the roof. Carlotta had mentioned a lightning conductor that they could climb down. She had also suspended a rope from a tree that abutted the prison wall. Within minutes the two men were free. They split up immediately and never saw each other again.

Carlotta had obtained papers for her brother in the name of Franz Bohumin, a family friend who had died recently in a car accident. Using these false documents, Schroder fled to Salzburg, where he found work and a new girlfriend, Adda Lienzer. And there the scent went cold.

Laub was not as fortunate. A little over one year later, in April 1948, German judicial patience finally expired and he was led to the gallows.

Schroder continued to evade his captors. And he might have vanished forever had he not married Adda. Her ex-husband, Joseph Lienzer, ferociously jealous of his former wife, still entertained hopes of a reconciliation and he began making inquiries about her new husband. He discovered that Franz Bohumin's wife, Julika, was still alive. Furthermore, according to neighbors, she was a widow. Lienzer dug deeper and unearthed Schroder's deception. Gleefully, he contacted the police. Somehow news of Lienzer's intervention reached Schroder who, once again, took off.

April 1950 found him in Rome, at the church of Santa Maria dell' Anima, just off the Piazza Navono, long a magnet for Austrian pilgrims visiting Rome. It was here that Schroder bumped into two Tyrolese visitors. Pope Pius XII had designated 1950 as Holy Year and Schroder's two new acquaintances were praying for an audience with the pope. They also hoped to secure visas to stay in Italy.

Schroder, still calling himself Bohumin, ruefully explained that he had lost his passport. The two men had a suggestion. They produced the papers of a friend, who had been unable to travel at the last moment; maybe Bohumin could use these to obtain a new passport? Schroder immediately approached the Austrian consulate. Just days later, he was presented with a new passport in the name of Alois Pretschmer, a native of Innsbruck. With his newfound friends, Schroder now headed for Naples.

They were given shelter by the nuns of Santa Cecilia. In return, the three men did work around the convent. But Schroder soon became bored. He contacted Adda and asked her to join him, telling the nuns that she was his fiancée. However, the steamy nature of their reunion caused plenty of red faces at the convent, and they were ordered to leave. Shortly after this Adda was on her way back to Austria, disillusioned and vengeful over Schroder's womanizing.

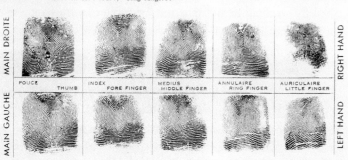

CONFIDENTIAL
Intended only for Police
and Judicial Authorities

BIGGS

Ronald, Arthur.

born on 8th August 1929 in BRIXTON/LONDON (Great Britain)
son of BIGGS given name not known
married to Renée ?
OCCUPATION : builder
NATIONALITY : British
IDENTITY HAS BEEN CHECKED AND IS CORRECT
DESCRIPTION : see photo and fingerprints, height 6'1", grey eyes, dark brown curly hair.
Scar on left wrist; long fingers.

MAIN DROITE — RIGHT HAND

| POUCE THUMB | INDEX FORE FINGER | MEDIUS MIDDLE FINGER | ANNULAIRE RING FINGER | AURICULAIRE LITTLE FINGER |

MAIN GAUCHE — LEFT HAND

FINGERPRINTED AND PHOTOGRAPHED IN LONDON (Great Britain) in 1963

PREVIOUS CONVICTIONS :
        This man has a long criminal record in GREAT
BRITAIN : convicted five times for robbery; twice
for receiving; twice for taking and driving away motor
vehicles without the consent of the owner; seven times
for breaking and entering and burglary; etc.---
After the GLASGOW-LONDON mail train robbery on 8/8/1963,
he was sentenced to 30 years' imprisonment; he escaped
from WANDSWORTH prison in London on 8/7/1965 with three
other prisoners.

MISCELLANEOUS INFORMATION :
        Was accompanied by : his wife; Robert Alves Anderson; Eric Flower; Patrick Doyle; Paul
Seabourne; Francis Victor Hornett.-- Could be in the company of other members of the gang which
robbed the mail train at Cheddington on 8/8/1963, are at large and are the subjects of the following
I.C.P.O.-INTERPOL international notices : EDWARDS Ronald, notice 555/63 A 4786 of September 1963;
REYNOLDS Bruce Richard, n°550/63 A 4782 of September 1963; WHITE James Edward, n°551/63 A 4783 of
September 1963; WILSON Charles, Frederick, n°517/64 A 5167 of November 1964.--- A warrant of arrest
will be issued shortly.--- EXTRADITION WILL BE REQUESTED.

REASON FOR THIS CIRCULATION :
        Done at the request of the BRITISH authorities in order to discover his whereabouts. If found
please detain and inform immediately : The British Representative, International Criminal Police
Organization, National Office, Criminal Investigation Department, New Scotland Yard, LONDON SW 1
(INTERPOL LONDON SW 1), and also : the I.C.P.O.-INTERPOL, General Secretariat, 37 bis rue Paul Valé-
ry, PARIS (INTERPOL PARIS).

I.C.P.O. PARIS
August 1965

File N° : 387/65
Control N° : A. 5408

An Interpol Red Notice for Ronnie Biggs, a British citizen and
infamous train robber, is displayed in the National Archives
in London, England, in 2005. A Red Notice was also used to
apprehend Manfred Schroder. *(Getty Images)*

It did not take Schroder long to find a replacement, named Rita. She introduced him to her family. She also assisted Schroder in his new guise of smuggler. Each night they would take a boat out to Capri, then sail north of Cape Miseno. There they would rendezvous with a contact, who handed over cartons of cigarettes. For several weeks all went well, but on the night of January 16, 1951, the contact failed to show. It was a similar story the following two nights. The next day Schroder was caught off guard when two police officers stopped him on the quayside and asked to see his papers. They told him that Holy Year was over and that the other two pilgrims had departed. Schroder, they explained, had overstayed his visa. He was bundled off to the local police headquarters, photographed, and fingerprinted, then freed on the condition that he leave the country within 48 hours.

Schroder suspected that he had been betrayed by Rita's brother, Claudio, who had hated him from the outset. He had also recently read that Interpol was now back in full operation. It could only be a matter of time, maybe hours, before his true identity was revealed. In desperation he turned to Rita. She handed over every penny she possessed and kissed Schroder goodbye.

Meanwhile, the net woven by Interpol had begun to tighten. Adda had told the police the name "Pretschmer," and he was traced to the convent. Then came a bombshell: Olga, Schroder's first wife, turned up alive and in Berlin. This made Schroder a bigamist twice over. And his problems kept multiplying. The man whose identity he had adopted in Rome, Alois Pretschmer, reported that he had lost his passport. The Austrian authorities insisted that he had been issued with a new one in Rome, which he denied. When the Viennese police contacted their Roman counterparts, they quickly wired the passport applicant's photograph back to Austria. There could be no doubt that it was Schroder, or Bohumin, or Pilger, or Pretschmer, or whatever name he was using.

Unraveling this web of deceit took time, and it was not until March 1951 that a Red Notice went out from Interpol that Manfred Schroder was wanted for murder, theft, and bigamy, among other crimes. The notice included a request for his extradition. Now all Interpol had to do was track him down.

(Continues on page 38)

FUNNY MONEY

Forgers like to consider themselves the most skillful of criminals, and the currency counterfeiter likes to regard himself as sitting atop the forging tree. The crime of counterfeiting currency dates back to the creation of money itself. The Roman emperor Nero (A.D. 37–68) is said to have been the first large-scale counterfeiter, minting coins of base metal covered with silver to deceive his own subjects. Since that time, most governments have metaphorically moved mountains in order to maintain the integrity of their national currency. This was especially true in the 1920s when the ICPC came into being. Fragile postwar economies, horror-stricken by the ruinous hyperinflation that destroyed Germany, could only imagine how much worse the problem might be if the counterfeiter played his hand. Even the stronger nations were not immune to this fear. (The U.S. Secret Service—the agency that protects the president—was actually founded in 1865 to suppress counterfeit currency.) Then, as now, the U.S. currency was the most counterfeited currency in the world. There are two reasons for this. American dollars are the closest thing the world has to an international currency. They are accepted in almost every country on Earth. The other big attraction for the counterfeiter is the dollar's uniform size. Every denomination—from a single dollar to $100—can be forged on the same size paper, although modern security strips built into the banknote have significantly added to the forger's problems. At its headquarters in Lyon, Interpol currently holds more than 15,000 different examples of counterfeit dollars.

When the ICPC was founded, its member states urged the organization to take strong action against counterfeiters, and in 1930 the ICPC responded by creating specialized departments to deal with currency counterfeiting, criminal records, and passport forgery. When Dressler assumed control, he took this one step further. He set up an anticounterfeiting section, which fell under the leadership of yet another Austrian,

Johann Adler. This was not a political appointment. Adler probably knew more about counterfeit currency than any man alive at the time. During his time at the helm—he retired in 1954—Adler oversaw publication of a quarterly called *Counterfeits and Forgeries Review*. Containing copies of the latest forgeries and bogus banknotes, this was circulated to every major police organization in the world and for years it was regarded as the foremost authority on currency counterfeiting.

Recent developments in photographic, computer, and printing technology have made the production of counterfeit money easier than ever. Interpol recognizes this. Today, instead of a quarterly magazine, Interpol makes its information available online via secure links that are available only to law enforcement agencies. If a phony banknote turns up in Japan, for example, within minutes of the Tokyo National Central Bureau informing Lyon, this information can be transmitted around the globe.

Interpol Secretary-General Ronald Kenneth Noble *(second from left)* participates in the First Global Congress on Combating Counterfeiting. Other participants include business leaders and public sector officials. *(AP Photo/Geert Vanden Wijngaert)*

(Continued from page 35)

Its strongest ally in this quest was Adda Lienzer. In June 1951 she again contacted the Austrian police, to tell them that Schroder was somewhere on the French Riviera and that he had secured a job on a motor yacht called *Santal* bound for America. A check of shipping agencies confirmed that a man calling himself Alois Pretschmer had signed on the *Santal*, but it was not Schroder. Unbeknownst to Adda— or anyone else at this juncture—Schroder had switched places with a crewmember of another vessel, the 104-ton schooner *Kangaroo*. And he had signed on with a passport in the name of a Walter Praxmarer.

MILLIONAIRE DAREDEVIL

The *Kangaroo*'s owner was Freddie McEvoy, a 43-year-old Australian-born playboy nicknamed "Suicide Freddie"[1] for his daredevil sporting exploits, which included racing cars and winning a bronze medal for bobsledding at the 1936 Winter Olympics, and who numbered movie star Errol Flynn among his close friends. In October 1951 McEvoy announced that the *Kangaroo* was heading to Nassau (in the Bahamas) for the winter social season. Schroder, aware by now that almost every police force in the world had his picture and fingerprints on record, jumped at this opportunity. Once in Nassau he was sure he would be safe (the Bahamas did not join Interpol until 1973). First, though, before braving the unpredictable Atlantic Ocean, the *Kangaroo* docked at Tangier, Morocco, for refitting.

The refit took longer than anticipated, and it was November before the *Kangaroo* set sail. A strong southwest gale forced the vessel to hug the Moroccan coast. This stretch of water could be deadly, and as the barometer plunged, the storm worsened. Huge waves tossed the tiny vessel around like a toy, destroying the rigging, and holing the boat below the waterline. A mad scramble for the inflatable life raft resulted in it capsizing, throwing all the occupants into the water. McEvoy, his wife Claude, 30, their 22-year-old maid Cecile Bruneau, and three crewmembers were all drowned. But not Schroder. He and two others, Willi Gehring and Franz Krotil, managed to right the life raft and fight their way to the lighthouse at Cap Beddouza, where they crawled ashore before collapsing with exhaustion.

It was here that Schroder's luck finally ran out. He and his fellow survivors muttered to each other in German, unaware that one of the lighthouse keepers understood every word. Mention of the word *smuggling*—later, there were unsubstantiated rumors that the *Kangaroo* had taken on contraband in Tangier—caught his attention. A quick phone call to the mainland did the rest. Detectives sailed out to the lighthouse, picked up the survivors, and took them to Rabat, where they were fingerprinted and asked for their names. Schroder gave his as Walter Praxmarer, saying that he was Austrian. When a check with Austria established that Praxmarer was really a dead soldier, the local commissar reached for his pile of Interpol red notices. One showed the photograph of Manfred Schroder, wanted for murder, robbery, and bigamy, and listed all his aliases. With his identity revealed, Schroder insisted that McEvoy had known about his antecedents. "I told him [McEvoy] everything," he told his captors. "He hired me and protected me."[2]

Over the next weeks and months the police forces of Morocco, Austria, Germany, Italy, France, Spain, Gibraltar, and Switzerland coordinated their extradition efforts through Interpol in Paris. Schroder's legal team fought them every step of the way, but they could not stave off the inevitable. With Berlin now a partitioned city, it was decided to try him in Austria, which was still under Allied occupation. In May 1954, at the Salzburg Court of Assize, Schroder was finally convicted of murdering Lotte Klinger. By this time Germany and Austria had abolished the death penalty, and Schroder was sentenced to 15 years imprisonment. The court added one codicil to the sentence: Schroder was ordered to be confined in a dark cell for 24 hours on October 3 every year—the anniversary of Lotte Klinger's murder.

Before the advent of Interpol it is likely that Schroder would have simply vanished, never to be seen again. As it was, it took more than eight years, but justice was finally done and the memory of that dreadful day in the Wannsee woods could be laid to rest.

The Phantom Shipment

Trying to unravel international fraud is never easy. Sometimes it can border on the impossible. It requires specialized knowledge of local banking regulations and customs, language skills, and a thorough understanding of extradition treaties. In short, it needs Interpol. This is why so much of Interpol's caseload is devoted to tracking down the international fraudster. Without Interpol, countries around the world would struggle to coordinate their efforts. Any kind of bureaucratic confusion is "money in the bank" to the financial trickster, who specializes in weaving a web of deception that can spread across international frontiers. Fraud can take many forms, but at the heart of each scam lies a single, crucial element: confidence. Everything hinges on the criminal gaining the complete trust of the victim. Once this has been achieved, the rest often falls into place with surprising ease.

In 1954 a gang of international fraudsters put together a scam of extraordinary complexity that fooled numerous sophisticated financial institutions. At the helm of this group of criminals was one of the 20th century's most remarkable lawbreakers, a man whose undoubted financial acumen never quite overcame the fact that he had the instincts and ethics of a street mugger. He could have been a successful businessman or entrepreneur, but instead he rotted away for years in various prison cells, toppled by his own arrogance and a refusal to consider the possibility that his pursuers might be just as smart, or smarter, than himself.

The wheels of this particular fraud were first set in motion on April 16, 1954, when the Kredietbank of Antwerp, the third-largest bank in Belgium and a soundly based institution that could trace its origins back to 1889, was asked by a Mr. Mayers, manager of a locally based firm of loss adjusters called Marinex, to arrange a credit account on behalf of the government of the Portuguese territory of Goa, in India. Recent civil unrest had led to food shortages and the government was desperate to feed its citizens. The $865,000 ($6.8 million in 2008) line of credit was intended to pay for a shipment of 5,000 tons of Italian rice and 3,000 tons of Burmese rice, for delivery to Goa's main port of Mormugao. The funds were to be made available to an Antwerp-based transport firm called Hantra.

Kredietbank liked the look of the deal and, on that same day, informed Hantra that it had opened this credit account in Hantra's name. The credit was to be valid until June 12, and the relevant documentation—bills of lading, the commercial invoice, the consular invoice, and the insurance policy—would be forwarded to the Kredietbank in due course. Such transactions were routine in the world of international commerce; the clients would get their rice, the vendors would get their money, and the bank that arranged the financing would earn a tidy commission on the deal.

A little more than a month later, on May 19, Hantra again contacted the Kredietbank. They said that the documentation would be handled by Modern Industries Ltd., a firm based in Colombo, the capital of Ceylon (now Sri Lanka). Hantra asked for the credit to be apportioned in the following manner:

1. $8,290 payable to Outshoorn and Landau, a firm of Antwerp underwriters that had agreed to insure the cargo
2. $669,860 to be transferred to the Banca Report of Lugano, Switzerland, in the name of George Kaufman
3. $6,850 to be retained by the Kredietbank and held at the disposal of Hantra

Two days later a letter confirming these arrangements was given to a Kredietbank official by a Mr. G. von Hornung, a resident of Basle who

(Continues on page 44)

HUNTING NAZIS

After the Second World War, many ex-Nazis fled Europe and sought sanctuary in South America. The most infamous of these was Josef Mengele, a doctor who conducted atrocious experiments on inmates at the Auschwitz-Birkenau concentration camp. Unfortunately, Interpol's appetite for pursuing war criminals was never very strong, but in May 1985 it finally issued a red notice seeking Mengele's arrest. It was already several years too late. The man branded the "Angel of Death" was dead; he had drowned on February 7, 1979, while swimming in Brazil. Ironically, confirmation of Mengele's death came less than one month after Interpol released its red notice.

Interpol figured far more prominently in the hunt for Josef Schwammberger, a Nazi SS officer responsible for hundreds of executions while he was commandant of three labor and concentration camps in Poland. After the war Schwammberger had been imprisoned in his native Austria, but he escaped in January 1948 from a train taking him to trial. Then he disappeared.

With so much Nazi-hunting attention centered on Mengele, lower-echelon killers dropped off the radar somewhat, but in January 1987 Interpol issued a red notice for Schwammberger, citing an arrest warrant for murder issued in Stuttgart, West Germany. Schwammberger was thought to be hiding in Argentina, a notorious safe haven for war criminals on the run, but West Germany's efforts to extradite him proved fruitless, and it was not until Interpol became involved that things started to happen. International pressure mounted on the Argentinean government with the discovery that Schwammberger was living in the La Plata region.

On November 13, 1987, police agents raided a ranch near the town of Huerta Grande. Schwammberger offered no resistance when arrested. This triggered a 30-month extradition battle as Schwammberger fought to remain in Argentina. But the government, aware that harboring known war criminals was severely damaging Argentina's global status and reputation, put him on a plane back to Frankfurt.

(continues)

Former Nazi labor camp commandant Josef Schwammberger is accompanied by a security officer upon arrival in Stuttgart, Germany, in May 1990. He was convicted and given a life sentence in 1992 for his role in the deaths of hundreds of Jews during his time at several labor camps. *(AP Photo/Thomas Kienzle)*

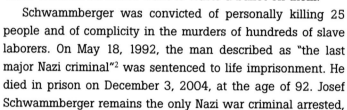

(continued)

After a lengthy delay, on June 26, 1991, the 79-year-old Schwammberger finally faced his accusers in a court of law. Witnesses described how he personally executed groups of Jews as they knelt beside mass graves, hurled emaciated prisoners onto bonfires, and smashed children's heads against walls "because he didn't want to waste a bullet on them."[1]

Schwammberger was convicted of personally killing 25 people and of complicity in the murders of hundreds of slave laborers. On May 18, 1992, the man described as "the last major Nazi criminal"[2] was sentenced to life imprisonment. He died in prison on December 3, 2004, at the age of 92. Josef Schwammberger remains the only Nazi war criminal arrested, tried, and convicted on an Interpol Red Notice.

(Continued from page 41)

also presented the required commercial invoice. On the following day, the Kredietbank received an official invoice, made out by the Portuguese consulate in Antwerp, attesting that the rice had had been loaded on May 13. The ship was a 5,805-ton freighter, the *Trianon*, belonging to the Wilhelmsen Line, a major Norwegian company that was represented in Antwerp by a shipping agency.

Mayers, meanwhile, discussed the arrangement with Outshoorn and Landau over several days. Everything seemed in order, and on May 21 they drew up the insurance policy and sent it to Kredietbank. The next day the bank had all the necessary documents in place. These were airmailed to Goa and, in accordance with instructions received from Hantra, the Kredietbank transferred to Lugano the sum of $669,860.

Three days later a man calling himself George Kaufman went to the Banca Report of Lugano and withdrew the cash sum of 1,571,874 Swiss francs, the equivalent of $366,860. He requested that the balance of $303,000 be transferred to the Hofmann Bank of Zurich, into the account of someone named Andre Klotz. Traditionally, Swiss banks have been very accommodating toward clients with unusual business requirements, and Hofmann silkily agreed when Kaufman asked them to arrange for a Zurich gold bullion firm to hand over to the bearer of a 1,000-lire Bank of Italy note—number 5/85/18364—four cases, each containing 16 bars of gold. Within hours, a man calling himself Klotz arrived at the bullion firm, presented the identifying banknote, collected the gold, and drove off.

THE SCAM REVEALED

One day later—May 26—the first uneasy rumblings began. The Kredietbank received a telegram from the Banco Nacional Ultramarino of Goa requesting the name of the cargo boat and its approximate date of arrival at Mormugao. The bank duly contacted the Antwerp representative of the Norwegian shipping firm. Their reply sent shockwaves through the Kredietbank: the *Trianon* was not carrying rice and was not scheduled to dock at Mormugao. A hasty telephone call to the Wilhelmsen Line head office in Oslo only confirmed this revelation. Immediately a telegram was wired to Lugano, blocking the $669,000. It arrived 24 hours too late. Every penny was gone.

The Kredietbank, aware it had been the victim of a major fraud, wasted no time in contacting the Belgian police. They quickly realized the enormity of this crime and immediately requested assistance from Interpol in Paris. Even their experienced fraud investigators were shocked by the scope and intricacy of a fraud that crossed five countries and two continents. At the urging of Interpol, detectives in Belgium slowly pieced together the background to the fraud. Mayers, the Marinex employee, was obviously a man they needed to interview as soon as possible. After all, it was Mayers who had first approached the Kredietbank, asking them to finance the shipping deal to Goa. And it was Mayers who had contacted the underwriters in connection with the insurance. Moreover, a search of the Marinex premises revealed several handwritten notes on the deal, many of which suggested that Mayers had been in correspondence with the Basle branch of Hantra, another company with its fingerprints on the fraud.

When arrested, Mayers seemed genuinely shocked. He protested that he knew nothing about the fraud. His only crime, he said, was to place his offices at the disposal of a Mr. G. von Hornung, the manager of the Basle branch of Hantra, and to help von Hornung prepare the paperwork for the Kredietbank. Immigration records confirmed that von Hornung had arrived in Antwerp from Basle on May 21 with three other men, one of whom spoke English and the other two French. A series of meetings was known to have taken place in the Marinex office.

Meanwhile, another team of detectives was investigating the documents presented to the Kredietbank. The bill of lading and the consular invoice were both false, though it took an expert to confirm this. The expert had rarely seen such workmanship. The official stamps and signatures would have deceived anyone outside the consulate. Forgeries of this caliber required not only impeccable craft, but also detailed knowledge of official procedures. Postwar Antwerp was a hotbed of forgery, and the police knew they would have a fiendish task in trying to track down the author of these phony documents. For this reason they decided to concentrate on Marinex's phone records. These showed that numerous calls had been made to London, Paris, Lugano, Basle, and Olten in Switzerland.

Interpol decided it was time to move. It contacted the Swiss police, and on June 5 swooped on the Basle branch of Hantra. Von Hornung was obviously stunned by their arrival and responded nervously to their inquiries. Two days later he was found dead, having committed suicide. The strain had been intolerable. By his body lay a signed statement revealing his part in the affair. In March 1954 he had been contracted by a Colombo firm, Modern Industries Ltd, with a business proposition. The deal sounded attractive and he agreed to act as an intermediary for this firm. On May 19 he had traveled to Paris to meet the representative of Modern Industries Ltd, a man called Savundranayagam, who presented documents from Colombo clearly authorizing him to act on behalf of the firm. The following day, von Hornung had traveled to Basle with Savundranayagam's assistant, an Englishman named Charles William Dade, to collect the commercial invoice, which he handed over to the Kredietbank.

Although shocked and temporarily stymied by von Hornung's suicide, the Swiss detectives switched their attention to Andre Klotz, the man who had collected the gold bullion in Geneva. Klotz was a reputable gold dealer and, when interviewed, denied all knowledge of the Antwerp scam. George Kaufmann had approached him in May, he said, looking to buy a quantity of gold. At this time, the private ownership of gold was illegal in many countries and such deals had to be done discreetly. On May 22 Klotz traveled to Lugano, Switzerland, with Kaufmann, and there met a Dr. Bera, adviser to the Banca Report. Klotz insisted that he had made a simple purchase of gold—perfectly legal in Switzerland—on behalf of a client, and nothing more. The police believed him. They now devoted all their efforts to finding Kaufmann. This turned out to be an alias; his real name was Ferdnand Geissman, a Swiss subject who was living in Paris. When French police went knocking at his door, however, they found no one at home.

THE YUGOSLAV CONNECTION

Eventually, Geissman surrendered to the authorities in Lugano. He said that in Paris he had been approached by two Yugoslavians, Miljusz and Sorz. They had asked him to go to Lugano, using a false name, to collect a large sum of money. He would be paid well for his time. In Lugano Geissman said he met with Dr. Bera, who gave him the false identity papers in the name of George Kaufmann and dispatched him to the Banca Report. His only task, he swore, was to hand over to Sorz on May 26 a portion of the money he had received in Lugano—1,160,000 Swiss francs. The previous day, acting on orders from Miljusz, he had given the balance—410,000 francs—to a lawyer in Olten, Switzerland, named Mr. Horn.

This story was checked by Interpol, which confirmed that Geissman did not see Mr. Horn, but rather someone impersonating him. The meeting took place in Horn's house, despite the provable fact that he was not home that day. Horn's son, who was present, recalled someone he identified as Geissman talking to a man he knew as a client of his father's, a Mr. Mniszek from Paris, and it was to him, he believed, that Geissman paid the money. Horn stated that he knew Mniszek through their mutual dealings with the firms of Hantra in Basle and Marinex of Antwerp. When Interpol cross-referenced its files, it noted that Mniszek was one of the names that had cropped up on Marinex's phone records in Antwerp.

One more link in this extraordinarily complicated chain came with the discovery that Mniszek made frequent visits to Antwerp, where he stayed with Mayers, and it was definitely established that he was in Antwerp on May 20 and had visited the Marinex office with his partners on that day. As Interpol collated all this information, they remained in constant touch with Belgian, Goan, French, Swiss, and Ceylonese police. The hunt was on for Mniszek, Sorz, Miljusz, and Bera.

In Antwerp the magistrates issued a warrant for the arrest of Mniszek and requested extradition. An Interpol "circulation" was sent through Paris to all the police in Europe and within a week Mniszek was picked up at the airport in Bordeaux. Shortly afterward, Bera and Sorz were both arrested in Paris, closely followed by Miljusz. The other participants—Geissman, Klotz, and Mayers—were all found to be innocent and released.

It took some time, but from this bewildering cast of characters Interpol isolated one name—Savundranayagam. Shadowy and elusive, he preferred to remain in the background while innocent patsies took all the risks, but there could be no doubt that his was the hand pulling the strings. Tracking him down took time. Then, in July, news came from Switzerland that Savundranayagam and another man had recently flown to England. Interpol promptly informed London that warrants had been issued in Belgium for their arrest. Three days later both men were arrested by detectives from Scotland Yard. After a lengthy inquiry, it emerged that the other man had been entirely duped by Savundranayagam, and he was subsequently freed and awarded costs for his inconvenience.

Interpol now devoted its efforts to shedding light on Savundranayagam's murky past. They discovered that his full name was Michael Marion Emil Anacletus Pierre Savundranayagam and he was born on July 6, 1923, the son of a judge in Ceylon. He was still in his early 20s when he developed an appetite for dubious business practices, and he quickly amassed a fortune by buying and selling surplus stores. His ability to turn a quick buck was undeniable, and so was his knack for bending the rules. In 1950 he was neck-deep in a deal in which a shipment of oil to China mysteriously vanished, along with a reported $1.2 million. Thereafter, banks in his home city of Colombo, Sri Lanka,

Savundranayagam, accompanied by his wife, makes his way to court in London, England, to answer for his fraudulent dealings as director of the Fire, Auto & Marine Insurance Company. Savundranayagam, at this point calling himself "Emil Savundra," was convicted in 1968. *(Getty Images)*

would have nothing to do with him. Shunned in his homeland, Savundranayagam shifted his base of operations to London, and it was from there that he orchestrated the Goa rice scam. Although Savundranayagam was arrested in July 1954, he managed to delay his extradition to Belgium by adopting what would become a favored device whenever apprehended by the law—feigning illness. Court sessions were held at Savundranayagam's bedside in the London Clinic, while lawyers wrangled over his future. (During this period, on December 16, 1954,

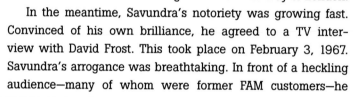

THE CRIMINAL PHOENIX

Several years after his release from prison, Savundranayagam once again hit the headlines. Back in London and now calling himself Emil Savundra, in 1963 he founded the Fire, Auto, and Marine Insurance Company (FAM). Savundra's lavish lifestyle, funded by a marked reluctance to pay any claims, led to discreet inquiries into his background. It emerged that he had been deported from Ghana in 1958 and, one year later, he had also fled Costa Rica, both times after swindling the government in business deals, and it soon became clear that FAM was yet another fraud. In 1966 the company collapsed, leaving thousands of policyholders without cover. As Scotland Yard struggled to untangle the mess—Savundra had always been a master of complexity—it requested the assistance of Interpol. A full dossier on Savundra's background made its way to London.

In the meantime, Savundra's notoriety was growing fast. Convinced of his own brilliance, he agreed to a TV interview with David Frost. This took place on February 3, 1967. Savundra's arrogance was breathtaking. In front of a heckling audience—many of whom were former FAM customers—he

he was also convicted in his absence by a French court on charges of exchange control violations and given a suspended prison term of three years.) Eventually, in February 1955, Savundranayagam ran out of legal arguments and was extradited to Belgium.

His erstwhile partners—Mniszek, Miljusz, and Sorz—all received token sentences (Bera was acquitted). None of the money or gold was ever recovered and the identity of the forger, whose false documents made the fraud possible, remained a mystery known only to the defendants.

This left Savundranayagam to face the music alone. Convicted on three charges of forgery and one count of swindling, he received a five-year prison term and a fine of 40,000 francs. True to form, he again

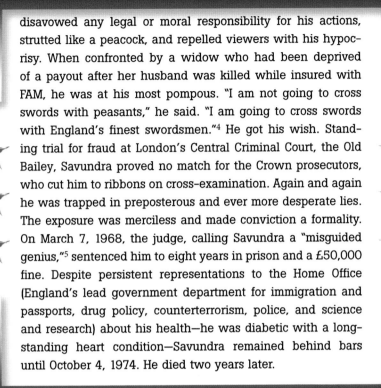

disavowed any legal or moral responsibility for his actions, strutted like a peacock, and repelled viewers with his hypocrisy. When confronted by a widow who had been deprived of a payout after her husband was killed while insured with FAM, he was at his most pompous. "I am not going to cross swords with peasants," he said. "I am going to cross swords with England's finest swordsmen."[4] He got his wish. Standing trial for fraud at London's Central Criminal Court, the Old Bailey, Savundra proved no match for the Crown prosecutors, who cut him to ribbons on cross-examination. Again and again he was trapped in preposterous and ever more desperate lies. The exposure was merciless and made conviction a formality. On March 7, 1968, the judge, calling Savundra a "misguided genius,"[5] sentenced him to eight years in prison and a £50,000 fine. Despite persistent representations to the Home Office (England's lead government department for immigration and passports, drug policy, counterterrorism, police, and science and research) about his health—he was diabetic with a long-standing heart condition—Savundra remained behind bars until October 4, 1974. He died two years later.

fell ill. When his appeal was dismissed in July 1956, his illness became markedly worse. On Sept 5, 1956, he was freed from prison on medical grounds, after having served just 15 months. According to someone who knew him well, Savundranayagam had engineered a heart attack, brought on by "a pill smuggled into prison."[3]

Washing the Money

Drug trafficking is the single biggest challenge that confronts Interpol. In terms of global economic impact, the sale of illegal narcotics dwarfs every other crime. According to the United Nations Office on Drugs and Crime, the annual value of the world's drug trade is approximately $320 billion.[1] (Comparing this to the estimated $1 billion generated by the sale of illegal firearms reveals just how immense the drug problem really is.) When talk gets around to the so-called war on drugs, it is easy to overlook the spin-off crimes that this industry spawns. People smuggling, organized prostitution, and travel-document counterfeiting are just some of the crimes financed by drug profits. And there is plenty of evidence to show that terrorist organizations have turned to drug trafficking, lured by the promise of colossal returns for a minimal financial outlay.

Sitting at the peak (in terms of profits) of the narcotics heap is cocaine. Although Interpol has monitored increases in cocaine usage around the world, the primary market remains the United States. Whether processed and sold on the street as crack or found in sugar bowls at swanky Hollywood parties, cocaine touches every socioeconomic group in America. And it is expensive. Deep in the jungles of Peru or Colombia—the two main producers—a kilo of coke costs around $3,000. By the time it has made the 3,500-mile journey to Los Angeles, the price has soared to $20,000. Every extra mile means extra risk and extra money. On the streets of New York or Chicago, that same kilo of coke will be worth $30,000 or more. Because nobody puts these kinds of purchases on their credit card, cocaine generates more physical cash than any other product in the world—so much, in fact, that getting the money out of America has always proved more difficult for the drug traffickers than getting the cocaine in.

Early one morning in January 1988 at Los Angeles International Airport, an employee of Loomis Armored Transport Co. was checking a shipment that had arrived overnight from a United Parcel Service (UPS) aircraft, when he noticed that one of the boxes was damaged. According to the shipping label, the box contained "gold scrap" being sent from a New York jewelry store to a Los Angeles gold dealer named Ropex. Yet when the Loomis employee went to reseal the torn package, he noticed that it felt very light, much lighter than it should be if it contained gold. He examined the carton more closely, peering inside. What he saw was not gold, but neatly bundled stacks of U.S. currency, amounting to $800,000, all in small bills. A quick check of the shipping manifest confirmed that the contents were supposed to be gold.

The puzzled employee took his concerns to his bosses. They thought it sounded odd and called Ropex's office in the Hill Street district, a 12-block area of downtown Los Angeles that is home to hundreds of jewelry outlets. Ropex did not sound unduly perturbed. There had probably just been an error on the manifest, an official said. The delivery was supposed to contain currency—cash that had been transferred from the East Coast to take advantage of higher short-term interest rates available at a local West Coast bank. The label was merely to protect the cash from the possibility of theft in transit.

Loomis had been in business for more than a century. During that time it had become a sophisticated international corporation, handling many unusual shipments, and it knew that Ropex's answer did not make sense. Any company so eager to extract the last decimal point of interest would have transferred the money electronically. This was not just easier and faster, but also much safer than shipping bulky boxes of cash from one side of the United States to the other.

A CURIOUS COINCIDENCE

Still not satisfied, Loomis went back and checked its records. Ropex was a regular client, and Loomis noticed that on days when it had made a delivery to the jewelry business, Loomis had also often transported very large sums of cash from Ropex to local banks later that same day. The amounts had ranged as high as $2 million. Something was not right. After an internal meeting, Loomis decided to deliver the shipment to Ropex. It also called the FBI.

Unbeknownst to the FBI, another government agency, the Internal Revenue Service (IRS), already had the Hill Street jewelry district on its radar. In late 1987 Wells Fargo Bank had noted unusual amounts of cash moving through a checking account at one of its suburban Los Angeles branches. A special watch was put on the account. By November of that year the numbers had become too big to ignore. After just three months of trading, a gold brokerage firm called Andonian Brothers had moved $25 million through its account. No other company in the Hill Street

THE BUSINESS OF DRUGS

When it comes to tackling the problems posed by drugs, Interpol, like every other law enforcement agency in the world, is always playing catch-up. As fast as one drug ring is shut down, another opens in its stead. And it is the same with cultivation. A concerted effort against the coca leaf producers in the Andean region has seen the land area given over to cocaine production in Colombia decline in recent years—by 52 percent in acreage between 2000 and 2006.[2] However, this has not had a significant impact on the amount of cocaine that Colombia exports to the rest of the world. Coca leaf production has simply been outsourced to neighboring Bolivia and Peru; production in these countries is up by 18 and 8 percent, respectively. Improved yields and enhanced production techniques have also helped maintain supplies at previous levels and kept the cartels rolling in cash.

With such enormous profits on tap, the cartels' budget for "research and development" rivals that of many multinational corporations. Most of this money goes into finding new methods of transporting drugs from one country to another. At one jewelry district was handling such huge sums of money. These kinds of numbers were more commonly associated with a world-renowned jewelry store such as Tiffany in New York, not a mom-and-pop outfit in downtown Los Angeles. Eventually, Wells Fargo decided to telephone the IRS.

By law, U.S. financial institutions have to report cash deposits of more than $10,000. At the time of this investigation, more than 7 million such deposits a year were being reported to the government. Trying to keep tabs on all these deposits was an impossible task. Here, though, the fact that two separate and highly reputable companies—Loomis and Wells Fargo—had both pointed the finger at the Los Angeles jewelry district attracted governmental minds. Curiosity soon grew into hard suspicion as, over the next 13 months, the FBI, the IRS, the Drug

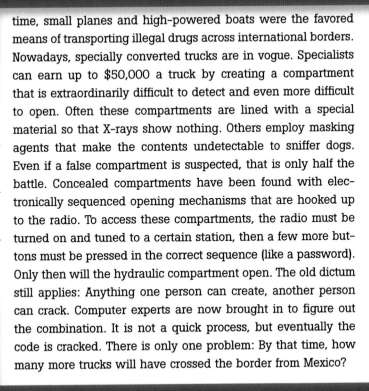

time, small planes and high-powered boats were the favored means of transporting illegal drugs across international borders. Nowadays, specially converted trucks are in vogue. Specialists can earn up to $50,000 a truck by creating a compartment that is extraordinarily difficult to detect and even more difficult to open. Often these compartments are lined with a special material so that X-rays show nothing. Others employ masking agents that make the contents undetectable to sniffer dogs. Even if a false compartment is suspected, that is only half the battle. Concealed compartments have been found with electronically sequenced opening mechanisms that are hooked up to the radio. To access these compartments, the radio must be turned on and tuned to a certain station, then a few more buttons must be pressed in the correct sequence (like a password). Only then will the hydraulic compartment open. The old dictum still applies: Anything one person can create, another person can crack. Computer experts are now brought in to figure out the combination. It is not a quick process, but eventually the code is cracked. There is only one problem: By that time, how many more trucks will have crossed the border from Mexico?

Enforcement Administration (DEA), and the U.S. Customs Service coordinated efforts to unearth just what was going on at Ropex and Andonian Brothers.

As the investigation's scope broadened, and it became clear that this was an international scam, the American agencies decided to call on Interpol's resources. From Interpol's records, they were able to obtain biographical information on the Andonian brothers.

Syrian-born Vahe Andonian was 24 years old when he immigrated to the United States in 1976 from Lebanon. Swapping war-shattered Beirut for the delights of Los Angeles was a head-turning experience for Vahe, one that he was eager to share with his younger brother. Nazareth Andonian, 21, an experienced diamond setter, joined Vahe that same year. With this kind of background it was no surprise that the brothers gravitated instinctively toward the Hill Street jewelry district, where they prospered. By 1979 they had accumulated enough capital to begin manufacturing gold jewelry on their own. They also began selling bulk gold, wholesale and retail.

At some point in the 1980s the Andonians were approached by another jewelry store owner, Wanis Koyomejian, who ran Ropex. He had a proposition for them. What Koyomejian had to say would eventually lead to the exposure of the largest money-laundering scam that the world had ever seen. It was so lucrative that its operators, the bosses of the Colombian Medellín drug cartel, nicknamed it La Mina: Spanish for "the Mine." Investigations would reveal that La Mina had been in existence for five years before the authorities first learned about it, and that its tentacles stretched around the world. Its specialty was moving money discreetly out of the United States. For a commission of 7 percent, La Mina boasted that it could repatriate funds from America to any country in the world in as little as 48 hours.

The money-laundering unit at Interpol in Lyon had seen nothing like it. Nor had anyone else, for that matter. Over its five-year existence, La Mina laundered an estimated $1.2 billion in cocaine profits out of the United States. To achieve this staggering figure it employed a variety of ingenious schemes, one of which involved Ropex and Andonian Brothers.

IDENTIFYING THE CRIMINAL MASTERMIND

It was all the brainchild of Raul Silvio Vivas, an Argentinean precious metals dealer and bank owner who lived in Montevideo, Uruguay. In 1985 Vivas began exporting gold to the United States. This was odd because, at the time, Uruguay had no gold-producing facility (the country's only gold mine, San Gregorio, did not become operative until 1997). This did not deter Vivas. His "gold" bars were actually lead, plated with just enough of the precious metal to fool casual inspection. He shipped these bars to Ropex and Andonian Brothers, who then sold the so-called gold to other jewelry outlets in Los Angeles, Miami, New York, and Houston—all hotspots in the cocaine trade.

Each consignment was paid for in cash—money that had accrued from countless street sales of cocaine in various cities. All the jewelry outfits involved were as phony as Ropex and Andonian Brothers. They were merely fronts for a sophisticated drug-trafficking operation, and their job was to "wash" the dirty money and ship it back to Los Angeles, for onward transmission to South America.

Through this ruse, millions of dollars from all over the country poured into the offices of the two Los Angeles firms every week. Armored trucks were turning up by the hour to transport the money to local banks. Some financial institutions were seriously concerned by this development and began asking questions. They realized that the jewelry business, with its high-priced items, generated huge sums of money, but why were these million-dollar deposits always in cash? The answer was glibly given. By dealing in cash alone, they said, both firms were protecting themselves against sudden and unexpected gyrations in spot-market precious-metal prices. It just did not smell right, and a few banks, such as Wells Fargo, pulled the plug on any future dealings with Ropex and Andonian Brothers. Other financial institutions, however, were not as inquisitive or discriminating. This laxity allowed hundreds of millions of dollars to flood into the Los Angeles banking system, most of which was held on short-term deposit until it was transferred by wire to accounts in Panama, and from there to banks in South America.

After a few months, Vivas realized that he did not even have to export phony bars to Los Angeles. It became entirely a paper transaction, with Ropex and Andonian Brothers "buying" gold that they never received but for which they were duly invoiced, and then "selling" it on to their outlets in the United States, which also never received it—but for which they paid with real money that of course ended up, all freshly laundered, in Colombia.

First, though, it had to pass through Los Angeles. After the Loomis and Wells Fargo tip-offs, undercover agents planted wiretaps on the phones at both Ropex and Andonian Brothers. They also installed concealed CCTV (closed-circuit television) cameras in both offices. What they saw astonished them: pallet loads of U.S. currency, money-counting machines working 24/7 just to keep up, and stacks of bills four-feet high. Bills less than $20 were simply tossed into a pile, too insignificant to count. There was so much money sloshing about that the counters could be heard complaining constantly about their workload.

Four Interpol NCBs—in Washington, Colombia, Uruguay, and Panama—coordinated the flow of information about La Mina and fed it back to the various American law enforcement agencies that were running "Operation Polar Cap," as it became known. (The name was coined from a government initiative to "freeze" the drug-traffickers' money.)

The agencies were in no rush to close down the money-laundering ring; they knew they had to build a cast-iron case if they wanted to defeat the army of high-priced lawyers that the criminals would undoubtedly field against them in court. From April to July 1988, the FBI carefully picked through documentation discarded by Ropex, looking for evidence of money laundering. They found tags from two bank currency bags that had contained $480,000, all in $20 bills. A search of Loomis's records showed that this very same amount had been delivered by Loomis to the Federal Reserve Bank some 18 days earlier. More sifting disclosed that Koyomejian controlled five separate companies in Los Angeles, Houston, and New York.

The key breakthrough came on January 25, 1989, when a telephone tap on the phone line at Andonian Brothers recorded a cryptic call from New York. The message was brief, "Four kilos eight six nine are on their way."[3] Agents understood immediately the significance of this coded message. From similar previous calls, they knew it meant that $4,869,000 had been dispatched. This was the largest single consignment of cash yet.

Interpol agents escort a drug trafficker to Simon Bolivar airport in Caracas, Venezuela. The man, Harold Gamboa Valasquez, was arrested at the request of Interpol and deported to Colombia. *(AFP/Getty Images)*

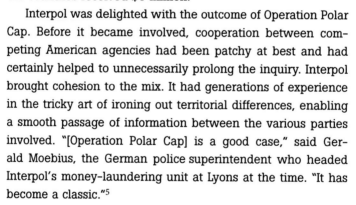

OPERATION POLAR CAP

By the time Operation Polar Cap was finished, 1,035 bank accounts and 179 banks had been investigated. It was therefore no surprise when, in a joint statement issued by American Attorney General Dick Thornburgh and Treasury Secretary Nicholas Brady, they described the 13-month Operation Polar Cap investigation as "the biggest of its kind ever undertaken by the government."[4] It led to the first conviction of a foreign financial institution—Banco de Occidente (Panama)—for violating U.S. money-laundering laws. As a direct result of this operation, over 100 people were arrested and more than $105 million in assets, including currency, bank accounts, real estate, jewelry, gold, and vehicles, was seized. The money forfeited by the Banco de Occidente (Panama) was shared with other governments, including Canada and Switzerland. Each of the countries received $1 million.

Interpol was delighted with the outcome of Operation Polar Cap. Before it became involved, cooperation between competing American agencies had been patchy at best and had certainly helped to unnecessarily prolong the inquiry. Interpol brought cohesion to the mix. It had generations of experience in the tricky art of ironing out territorial differences, enabling a smooth passage of information between the various parties involved. "[Operation Polar Cap] is a good case," said Gerald Moebius, the German police superintendent who headed Interpol's money-laundering unit at Lyons at the time. "It has become a classic."[5]

MILLIONS OF DOLLARS

That night, a U.S. Customs team boarded a UPS cargo aircraft in New York. Loomis had space reserved on this plane. Among its payload was a 30-box shipment from a New York jewelry shop, scheduled for delivery to Los Angeles and Andonian Brothers. When agents opened the shipment they found tightly packed bundles of currency in denominations as small as five dollars. The total, as promised, was $4,869,000. The shipment was immediately seized.

When the packages did not arrive the next day, Andonian Brothers was struck by a nasty case of the jitters. Nazareth Andonian phoned Loomis, desperate to locate his missing shipment. He was told that no such order existed. This sparked a string of panicky calls to the New York jewelers who had made the shipment. They, of course, insisted that the shipment had left them as scheduled. Finally, with his head in a spin, Andonian mustered the courage to call Montevideo to speak with Vivas. It is fair to say that Vivas was not pleased by the news.

Oddly enough, though, the alarm bells did not ring loudly enough for the Andonian brothers to close down their operation. Instead, they conducted business as usual, which would cost them dearly. On February 22, almost a month later, they were still in Los Angeles when teams of federal agents swept through the Hill Street jewelry district, arresting not just the Andonians but Wanis Koyomejian (the owner of Ropex) as well. Simultaneous raids in Texas, Florida, and New York netted a further 32 suspected members of the money-laundering ring. Also seized in the raids were 640 pounds of cocaine and more than $65 million in banknotes.

That same day the Interpol NCB in Uruguay issued what is known as a "diffusion"—or All Points Bulletin—for Raul Vivas, and followed it up with a formal red notice requesting his arrest. He was taken into custody in Montevideo, pending extradition to the United States. According to his lawyer he was "a world-renowned and highly respected precious-metals dealer"[6] who was innocent of any wrongdoing. The American authorities saw Vivas in a rather different light. As one FBI spokesman put it, "Vivas is probably the top money launderer to the cartels, or very close to the top."[7] Vivas fought tooth and nail to remain in Uruguay, but on December 9, 1989, he was put on a plane and flown back to the United States to stand trial with his erstwhile business associates.

On December 27, 1990, Vivas, the Andonians, and another man, Juan Carlos Seresi, who, according to prosecutors, helped ship the money to the Andonians, were convicted of laundering drug profits. Sentencing was delayed until the following year. On August 21, 1991,

U.S. District Judge William Keller told the men, "This kind of conduct cannot and will not be tolerated."[8] Vivas, 41, described as the creator of the scheme; Nazareth and Vahe Andonian; and Juan Carlos Seresi were each sentenced to 505 years in prison without the possibility of parole. In addition, Vivas was fined $7 million and the Andonians $1.7 million each.

In separate proceedings, in October 1993, Koyomejian agreed to plead guilty to charges of money laundering in return for a 23-year sentence. He was released on January 29, 2007.

The
Boiler Room

In the late 1980s Interpol was in danger of being swamped by an unprecedented rise in so-called white-collar crime. Requests for assistance were streaming in from around the globe. One of Interpol's divisions, then called the Fraud and Economic Crime Group (FECG), was determined to get a handle on this upsurge, and drew up a list of no fewer than 30 different types of international business crime. These included land investment fraud, commodity scams, snake oil salesmen peddling dubious timeshares, maritime frauds, counterfeit credit cards, and bogus airline tickets. On a daily basis the FECG was dealing with international scams that totaled in the billions of dollars. And yet the department was expected to combat this tidal wave of crime with a staff that numbered just four investigators.

It was all a question of priorities. Interpol had surveyed the crime landscape and reached a decision—that people getting their life savings ripped off mattered less than the war on drugs. Sven-Erik Ladefoged, who headed the FECG at the time, was under no illusions about where his department stood in the pecking order: "People die of drugs," he said, "but no one dies of economic crime,"[1] hence the skimpy, almost laughable staffing levels.

Adding to the problem is the sheer complexity of investigating economic crime. Very few police officers have a background in financial analysis. Understanding balance sheets (which provide a summary of a company's financial assets and liabilities), prospectuses, share offerings, and other similar matters requires an in-depth, specialized knowledge that is simply unavailable without special training. Seemingly ignorant of this basic fact, the FECG adopted the same revolving door policy to staff as does the rest of Interpol. Officers are drawn from the various

NEW HEADQUARTERS

On May 17, 1986, Interpol headquarters at St. Cloud, in Paris, came under attack from terrorists. A commando unit sprayed gunfire, wounding a police guard, and then made a failed attempt to blow up the building with explosives. An extremist left-wing group calling itself Direct Action claimed responsibility for the raid. With such attacks on official buildings becoming ever more prevalent, the incident merely reinforced Interpol's need to search for a new home. Traditionalists favored keeping the headquarters in Paris, but the mayor of Lyon, France's "second city," had other ideas. He wanted the prestige of having Interpol in his municipality and dangled an irresistible carrot: a handsome two-and-a-half acre site on the banks of the River Rhône, assistance with removal expenses, and a nominal rent. Construction began in July 1987. A shade over two years later, on November 28, 1989, the gleaming, five-story glass and concrete edifice at 200 quai Charles de Gaulle was ready for occupation. It was opened by French president François Mitterrand. Outside, the building is surrounded by a moat and a series of high fences and topped with three huge antennae, designed to handle more than 1 million messages a year. Inside, with its smoked-glass windows, a skylighted atrium ringed by potted plants, and panoramic views of the Rhône, it looks more like a corporate headquarters than a law enforcement agency. But appearances can be deceiving. Interpol's new headquarters, packed with the very latest in computer technology, had been purpose-built to be the most modern police headquarters on Earth. At long last, Interpol had a home befitting its status as the world's premier international crime fighting organization.

Interpol's headquarters was moved to Lyon, France, after its Paris headquarters was attacked by terrorists in 1986. *(AP Photo/Laurent Cipriani)*

member nations on a rotational basis, and once their term of office expires, they return to their home forces. This egalitarianism is all well and good when it comes to dealing with general crime or drugs, but it takes a year or more to train someone in the ways of white-collar crime, and by that time the trainee is scheduled for transfer. Another face shows up and the learning process has to begin all over again. Despite this less than ideal backdrop, the FECG somehow managed to pull off near-miracles. One of these triumphs occurred in 1988, when the unit helped to shut down one of the largest swindles in European history.

Mougins, on the Côte d'Azur in southern France, has been home to some of the world's most celebrated people. Pablo Picasso lived here for the last 15 years of his life; other regulars included Winston Churchill, fashion designer Christian Dior, and the movie star Catherine Deneuve. It is not difficult to see why they come. The village, with its winding, narrow streets, nestles in the hills above Cannes and enjoys glorious views out over the glistening Mediterranean. Tucked away between Mougins's 40 restaurants and 18 art galleries is some of the most expensive real estate in the world. The houses are magnificent and very private—just what Thomas F. Quinn wanted.

In the late 1980s this Brooklyn-born former attorney seemed to have it all: a $6.5 million mansion in Mougins, complete with Roman pillars and a waterfall on the grounds; a gorgeous woman by his side; yachts and a private jet; an apartment on the fashionable Avenue Foch in Paris; and a personal fortune that many believed put him well on the road to billionaire status. On the morning of July 27, 1988, he also received a visit from the French police. They had descended on Mougins at dawn, looking more like commandos than gendarmes. Squads of officers rushed the Quinn residence, a pink stucco villa called Le Mas des Roses (the Manor of the Roses). There was no resistance from the occupants.

RAIDS ACROSS EUROPE

In three other raids that morning—all synchronized—police in West Germany, Switzerland, and elsewhere in France netted another 21 suspects with connections to Quinn. All were charged with fraud and securities manipulation. As the 51-year-old Quinn and his longtime companion, Rochelle Rothfleisch, were driven away from Mougins in handcuffs to the notoriously tough La Santé Prison in Paris, he was probably not too perturbed. Getting arrested was something that Quinn had gotten used to over the years.

His brushes with the law had begun in 1963, when he was president of a small Wall Street brokerage company called Williams, Thomas and Lee Inc. He was still only 26 and just three years out of law school, but Quinn was hungry for money and he did not mind cutting corners. He got caught selling unregistered securities in a company called Kent Industries, a virtually worthless Florida land development with a negative balance sheet and no operations. Then came another dubious venture, involving a conflict of interests over a stock offering for a string of bagel shops. It turned out that, while Quinn was representing the brokerage firm underwriting the deal, one of his partners was acting for the bagel company. This was too much for the Securities and Exchange Commission (SEC), the industry watchdog for stock-related irregularities, and it filed charges. In 1970 Quinn was convicted for his part in both operations. His sentence was emphatic. He was barred from appearing before the SEC; barred from associating with securities firms; barred from practicing law in New York; and he received a six-month prison term in the Danbury Federal Correctional Institute in Connecticut. Upon his release, Quinn returned to the bagel business and, according to an FBI investigation report from the early 1980s, began consorting with known mobsters. The report describes Quinn as an "LCN (La Cosa Nostra) associate."[2] The SEC continued to monitor Quinn and, in 1980, he once again popped up on their radar when he was linked to the flotation of a Nevada company called Sundance Gold Mining and Exploration. Stock in the company climbed after it announced a major gold find in Surinam, only for the SEC to suspend all trading in Sundance when it emerged that the statement was bogus. Quinn stalled for years and, in the end, without admitting any guilt, managed to settle with the SEC in 1986. Then, working on the principle that the United States was getting a little too hot for comfort, he uprooted his entire operation and moved to the South of France.

It was shortly after this that he first came to the attention of Interpol. National Central Bureaus, or NCBs, are Interpol's foothold in each member country. It is the job of the NCB to act as the designated contact point for the General Secretariat in Lyon, submitting information, acting on information received, and facilitating extradition requests. In the early part of 1987, Interpol began receiving reports from NCBs—in countries as far apart as Brazil, Britain, the United Arab Emirates, Hong Kong, and Australia—of stock-trading scams that bore suspiciously similar characteristics to one other.

It all began with a newsletter. The names varied—the Strategy Market Letter, the Swiss Analyst, or Flash Report—but what they all shared were high production values. These were not shoddy, photocopied sheets, but rather sleekly designed and expensively printed brochures packed with what appeared to be top quality research on stock market

(Continues on page 71)

GETTING THE MESSAGE

Interpol is all about information. It was created to facilitate the smooth exchange of data across international borders, and that is still its primary function. It achieves this via an impressive bank of databases. These include the following:

Notices: This is the core system in which Interpol alerts police forces around the world about fugitives, suspected terrorists, dangerous criminals, missing persons, or weapons threats. In 2007 more than 5,000 arrests were made on the basis of a notice or diffusion (a similar but less formal type of alert).

Nominal Data: This contains approximately 178,000 records of known international criminals, missing persons and dead bodies, with their criminal histories, photographs, fingerprints, and the like.

International Child Sexual Exploitation Database (ICSE DB): This successor to the Child Abuse Image Database (ICAID) is very tightly controlled—it cannot be accessed remotely—and holds more than 520,000 images submitted by member countries. Sophisticated image recognition software connects images from the same series of abuse or the same location.

Stolen and Lost Travel Documents: This database contains information on more than 8 million passports and 6 million travel documents reported lost or stolen by 133 countries. It enables Interpol's National Central Bureaus and other authorized law enforcement entities (such as immigration and border control officers) to ascertain in seconds the validity of a suspect travel document. It is the only database of its kind in the world and is regularly accessed by security agencies at airports and seaports in the United States. Each month it processes between 10,000 and 12,000 messages from member states.

Stolen Administrative Documents: This database contains information on almost 190,000 official documents that serve to identify objects, such as vehicle registration documents and clearance certificates for import/export.

Stolen Motor Vehicles: A rapidly growing database, this provides extensive identification details on approximately 4.7 million vehicles reported stolen around the world. In recent years there has been a significant rise in the number of high-value cars being stolen to order and then shipped halfway around the world for resale. In 2007 more than 3,000 stolen motor vehicles a month were identified using the database. This is a fast-growing crime, with many vehicles destined for Africa and the Gulf States.

Stolen Works of Art: This allows member countries to research records on nearly 32,000 pieces of artwork and cultural heritage that have been reported stolen all over the world.

DNA Profiles: In 2002 Interpol began gathering DNA data from swabs collected at crime scenes internationally. Currently, the database contains around 77,000 DNA profiles from 47 countries. DNA profiles are numerically coded sets of genetic markers unique to every individual and can be used to help solve crimes and identify missing persons and unidentified bodies.

Fingerprints: Like most law enforcement agencies, Interpol uses an Automated Fingerprint Identification System (AFIS). This contains about 80,000 sets of fingerprints and 1,000 crime scene marks. Previously, matching fingerprints was an arduous, time-consuming process; it was performed manually and could take days or even weeks to find a match. Computerization

(continues)

(continued)

and AFIS have changed all that. Now, any possible matches are flagged in seconds. Full identification, though, is still left to human experts. Member countries submit fingerprints and crime scene marks either electronically or by mail.

Counterfeit Payment Cards: This database holds images of counterfeit/cloned credit cards and corresponding data. Seized cards are categorized and form a standard reference library against which suspect cards can be checked.

Fusion Task Force: Probably the most controversial of Interpol's databases, this lists 9,000 known or suspected terrorists from 120 countries. Concerns center on the fact that many of the persons listed have not yet committed any crime.

A fingerprint expert in Interpol's fingerprint unit discusses a tsunami victim's fingerprint at a laboratory in Thailand in January 2005. *(Kin Cheung/Reuters/Landov)*

opportunities. These newsletters arrived in the mailboxes of lawyers, doctors, company executives, and wealthy retirees across Europe and into the Middle East. Many came with "free trial" subscriptions. Each month, regular as clockwork, the newsletters continued to arrive. Then came the follow-up phone call. The salesmen were very good. Most spoke with cultured American or British accents and their names were reassuringly impressive—Fleming Windsor, for example, or Charles Church. The titles of the companies they represented also inspired confidence—Falcontrust, Prudentrust, First Gibraltar Financial Consultants, and Equity Management Services. At first the sales pitch was decidedly low-key, usually extolling the virtues of solid blue-chip stocks such as IBM or Siemens. Gradually a rapport was built, with clients receiving personalized attention and even a card at Christmas. Then it was time to dangle the financial worm: "Of course, if you're looking for something a little more exciting . . . ?"

Most investors gobbled up the bait. What followed was a quick, painful, and very expensive introduction to the world of "penny stocks." Despite the name, penny stocks rarely cost just pennies and can sell for hundreds of dollars; what they all share in common is that they are extraordinarily difficult to sell. Unlike the stock of major listed companies, which is easily traded on exchanges around the globe, the market in penny stocks is perilously thin. Often it is made by a single brokerage firm. This company, alone, sets the buy and sell price, and it can charge whatever it likes in either direction. Nowadays, the dangers of penny stocks are well advertised, but in the late 1980s, few outside of Denver and Salt Lake City—traditionally the homes of these unregulated markets—had ever heard of them.

WORKING THE PHONES

It was this ignorance of penny stocks that Thomas F. Quinn relied upon. Interpol discovered that he had spun a web of "boiler rooms"—high-pressure telephone sales offices—that stretched the length and breadth of Europe. Within days of the penny stock literature being mailed out to clients, it was time to hit the phones. Victims who bought into this scam received formal certificates for the stocks they owned, along with an impressive-looking computer printout that listed their holdings.

Thereafter, salesmen would call repeatedly, saying how well the stocks were doing and recommending new purchases. Rumors of takeovers were a common method of piquing interest and ramping up the stock price. The salesmen even had a strategy if the investor wanted to sell his stocks. They told the customer that the stock had suddenly fallen below its purchase price and that selling now would entail taking a big financial hit. A much better idea would be for the brokerage firm to buy back the stocks at their original purchase price, and swap them for another, more exciting issue. As the new issue was always more expensive than the original stock, this required the investor to cough up even more money. Going down this road kept the investor locked in and constantly out of pocket.

At some point, though, the phone calls stopped coming. When the puzzled customer tried to get through to the brokerage house, all he heard was an automated message saying the line had been disconnected. Only then did the reality of the rip-off hit home. Disgusted and often fleeced of thousands of dollars, some were too embarrassed to complain; others were furious and determined to do something about it. Complaints began pouring into stock market regulatory bodies in France, Switzerland, and elsewhere.

This was where Interpol became involved. The NCBs soon spotted a recurring pattern of circumstances behind these complaints, which were forwarded to the General Secretariat. A special working party was convened at Interpol headquarters. Representatives jetted in from around the world to swap financial horror stories. Agents from the FBI and the IRS brought a full dossier on Quinn's background. Each day the extent of the fraud became more and more apparent. It was enormous. By the time the dust had settled, it became apparent that upward of 10,000 investors worldwide had been duped into handing over a total of $500 million. Switzerland, alone, had received 570 complaints from disgruntled citizens, while one Persian Gulf investor was reportedly bilked out of $750,000. Most of the money was thought to have disappeared into Quinn's pockets.

Interpol had seen nothing like it before. One investigator described the organization of the network as "amazingly intricate and worthy of any multinational corporation."[3] Quinn had developed an almost unbreakable maze of companies. There was one quirk that Interpol spotted early on. Although all the worthless companies that Quinn pushed were American-based, not a single victim of his scam lived in the United States. After his previous brushes with the American legal system, Quinn had deliberately avoided targeting suckers in his home country. He knew that if he were ever convicted again of securities fraud in the United States, it would mean years, possibly decades, behind bars. As it was, he had no expectations of ever being caught. He thought he had developed the perfect business plan, one that would allow him to open up boiler rooms anywhere in the world. As soon as any investigative heat became too intense, he could simply shut down the operation, move on, and begin somewhere else. Best of all was that there was no paper trail leading back to him. His tracks were covered. Or so he thought.

Like thousands of criminals before him, Quinn learned the hard way that there is no honor among thieves. In short, he was betrayed. Just hours before the police stormed Quinn's villa in the South of France, another visitor had departed rather suddenly. He was thought to have made his escape from the Côte d'Azur aboard a yacht. His name was Arnold Kimmes, a 67-year-old veteran of the boiler room scams and a longtime mentor of Quinn, and he was desperate to get back to America. Just weeks earlier, Kimmes been arrested on federal racketeering and securities fraud charges. Faced with the very real prospect of dying in prison, Kimmes began exploring the plea-bargain possibilities. The deal worked out as follows. Kimmes would serve a short term in a California prison and forfeit two yachts—worth $1.1 million and $125,000 respectively—to the U.S. government. In return, Kimmes blew the whistle on Quinn.

Getting Quinn behind bars was one thing; finding out what he had done with the money was next to impossible. Laurent Kasper-Ansermet, the Geneva investigating magistrate who headed the main Swiss inquiry, summed up Interpol's frustration: "It [the money] went through many bank accounts."[4] One of Quinn's destination banks was the notorious Bank of Credit and Commerce International (BCCI), which collapsed in 1991 amid claims of fraud, but there were scores of others in Switzerland, Gibraltar, and Luxembourg.

Although Interpol had coordinated an investigation that broke the back of the biggest stock manipulation scam that Europe had ever seen, the subsequent trial ended on a less than satisfactory note. On July 10, 1991, in Paris, Quinn was convicted of stock market fraud against 93 investors, and of using false passports. He was imprisoned for four years and fined 300,000 francs ($65,500). His erstwhile partner, Arnold Kimmes, was sentenced in absentia to five years in prison and a fine of 1 million francs ($212,590). Blaine Chambers, an American, was also convicted in absentia and given a three-year prison term and a fine of 100,000 francs ($21,259). Two other accomplices, Gary Reid of Canada and Hussein Moosa, an Indian, were sentenced to two years in prison and given fines of 100,000 francs apiece; again, neither defendant was present in court. Carl Davis of Britain, who was present for the proceedings, was given a six-month suspended jail sentence and fined 20,000 francs for illicit stock market operations, but was found not guilty of being an accessory to fraud. Quinn's partner, Rochelle Rothfleisch, was acquitted of being an accessory to fraud.

The Long-
Distance Killer

For the most part, serial killers are creatures of habit who operate within a geographical comfort zone. It is all a matter of familiarity. They get to know a region—where to select victims, where to dump bodies, how to avoid detection from prying eyes, and how to make a successful getaway. Although these killing zones may extend over many square miles—one particular freeway, for example—patterns begin to emerge, giving investigators something with which to work. The real difficulties kick in when the serial killer starts to ply his trade in different countries, even different continents. Police departments have notoriously limited jurisdictions. For some, the notion of information sharing with other law enforcement agencies, even in their own county, is a foreign concept. This is where Interpol comes in. Decades of smoothing ruffled political feathers between nations have made Interpol agents masters in the art of information interflow. With their secure communication networks, Interpol is able to transmit information, safely and instantly, to any part of the globe. Only through this mechanism is it possible to pursue the international serial killer from one country to the next, until he is behind bars. Indeed, without Interpol, many investigations into this fortunately rare type of murderer would never even get underway. In order to arrest an international serial killer, investigators first have to know that a serial killer is out there. It is Interpol that fills in the missing gaps.

On the morning of July 11, 1991, Fred Miller, a homicide detective with the Los Angeles Police Department (LAPD) had no doubt that he was hunting a serial killer. That day, the body of Sherri Long, a prostitute with several convictions, had been found in Malibu. She had been strangled with her own bra and had been dead for approximately seven days. Just over three weeks before, on June 19, another prostitute, 20-year-old Shannon Exley, had been found strangled in suspiciously similar circumstances: rural location, knotted bra, no witnesses. During the interim between these two crimes, Miller had seen a Teletype message about a third murder, this time of Irene Rodriguez, 33, in Hollenbeck, just east of downtown Los Angeles. Again, there was the killer's signature—a knotted bra. An expert on knots, criminalist Lynne

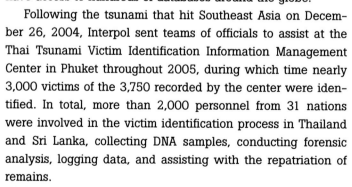

IDENTIFYING THE VICTIMS

Not all of Interpol's work deals with crime. An oft-overlooked role is the part that it plays in helping to identify the victims of large-scale tragedies. When a major disaster occurs, one country alone may not have sufficient resources to handle the processing of mass casualties. In some cases, the incident may have damaged or destroyed the country's existing emergency-response infrastructure, making the task of victim identification even more difficult. Interpol's role in such instances is crucial. Because the process of identifying victims of disasters, such as terrorist attacks or earthquakes, is rarely possible by visual recognition, it places a much greater responsibility on fingerprints, dental records, or DNA samples. By channeling this information through Interpol, investigators at the scene can have access to hundreds of databases around the globe.

Following the tsunami that hit Southeast Asia on December 26, 2004, Interpol sent teams of officials to assist at the Thai Tsunami Victim Identification Information Management Center in Phuket throughout 2005, during which time nearly 3,000 victims of the 3,750 recorded by the center were identified. In total, more than 2,000 personnel from 31 nations were involved in the victim identification process in Thailand and Sri Lanka, collecting DNA samples, conducting forensic analysis, logging data, and assisting with the repatriation of remains.

Herold, who worked for the Los Angeles County Sheriff's Department, had no doubt that all three ligatures had been tied by the same man.

Details of the killings were fed into the FBI's Violent Criminal Apprehension Program (VICAP) database, which has grown up on the principle that crime signatures—the manner in which serious crimes are committed—can be almost as unique as a fingerprint, with each killer displaying a distinctive quirk or pattern of quirks that highlight his individuality. Ordinarily, VICAP can be expected to generate the 10 closest matches from known previous crimes. In this case it drew a blank. The Los Angeles killings were so distinctive that they only

More recently, Interpol has been asked to assist in coordinating international efforts to identify the victims of the May 31, 2009, Air France plane tragedy in which 228 people from 32 countries lost their lives on a flight from Rio de Janeiro to Paris. When Flight 447 mysteriously crashed in stormy weather, it was hundreds of miles out in the Atlantic, making this, logistically, the most difficult search and recovery mission in aviation memory. An Interpol official was assigned to the French gendarmerie's crisis center in Paris, where efforts were conducted in accordance with Interpol's internationally accepted Disaster Victim Identification (DVI) protocols. As the bodies were found, experts concentrated on fingerprints, tattoos, surgical implants, and dental X-rays, which were then compared with dental and medical records, fingerprints, and DNA recovered from the victims' homes or provided by family members.

At the same time, Interpol's headquarters in Lyon remained in permanent contact with Brazilian authorities via its National Crime Bureau in Brasilia, coordinating all forms of assistance and placing the resources of the organization's 188 member countries at the inquiry's disposal.

As people travel more and more for business and leisure, the chances increase of a disaster that will result in the deaths of nationals from many different countries. It is in the midst of such tragedy that Interpol thrives.

resembled each other. Miller realized that he was up against a thoroughly professional serial killer who had struck three times within a 14-day period. If past experience was anything to go by, then it would only be a matter of time before he struck again.

EUROPEAN COUNTERPART?

Coincidentally, half a world away from Los Angeles, in Austria, the Viennese police were experiencing similar fears. Since the turn of the year, Vienna's red-light district had been paralyzed with fear. In the space of just a few weeks, beginning in April, four prostitutes had mysteriously disappeared. Their bodies began turning up on May 20. The first was found in Vienna Woods. The 25-year-old's name was Sabine Moitzi and she had been strangled with her own pantyhose and covered with leaves. She had been reported missing on April 16 and an autopsy indicated that she had been killed shortly thereafter. Three days later, in the same woods, another young woman, Karin Eroglu, also 25, was discovered. This time the strangler had used Eroglu's leotard as a ligature.

Dr. Ernst Geiger, who was leading the investigation into the disappearances, feared it would only be a matter of time before the other two missing women, Silvia Zagler and Regina Prem, were found dead. He did not know how to react. Countries like Austria are not accustomed to serial killers, which is why the murders caused such a furor in the Viennese press. Journalists began harrying the police for leads. One of the most persistent was a reporter for the Österreichischer Rundfunk (ORF), the Austrian Broadcasting Corporation. He arrived at police headquarters on June 3, 10 days after the first body was found, saying that he was producing a current affairs program for a respected radio station. He spoke to Police Chief Max Edelbacher about the murders, diligently taking notes throughout the interview. Two days later, when his program aired, it garnered good ratings and Edelbacher commented favorably on the program to his wife. The reporter had really made an impact on him, he explained, mainly because of his unusual—for an Austrian—first name, Jack. His full name, he said, was Jack Unterweger.

At this Edelbacher's wife looked askance at her husband. Didn't he know who Jack Unterweger was? she asked. Edelbacher just shrugged.

His incredulous wife went on to explain that Unterweger had once murdered a woman, but was now free. The newspapers had covered his extraordinary story in depth, citing Unterweger as a shining example of prison's rehabilitative powers.

He had been born in 1950 in Judenburg, a town in the Austrian state of Styria. His full name was Johann, but his mother, who claimed that the father was an American GI named Jack, preferred to call him by that name, and so did everyone else. Unterweger had a tough childhood. His mother was in and out of jail, and he was largely raised by an abusive grandfather. After a career of petty and not so petty crime, in 1975 he was convicted of murdering his 18-year-old neighbor, Margret Schafer, by strangling her with her bra. At his trial he claimed that visions of his mother's face flashed before him as he garroted the hapless Schafer. An expert witness, Professor Klaus Jarosch, who was asked to provide a psychological assessment of Unterweger for the court, described him as "an emotionally impoverished, explosive, aggressive psychopath . . . recidivism has to be expected with certainty."[1] As prophecies go, it was chillingly accurate.

When Unterweger entered Stein Prison on the banks of the Danube in Krems, Lower Austria, he was illiterate. By sheer force of personality he taught himself to read. Not only that, he also discovered a genuine talent for writing. He began submitting stories to the radio. Radio stations liked them and eventually broadcast around 50 of his works. From there, plays, poetry, and a novel flowed from his pen. All met with acclaim. In 1984 he received an Austrian literary award for his work *Endstation Zuchthaus* (Terminal Prison). The Viennese literati took him to their hearts, often attending his readings in prison, heralding him as a model of rehabilitation and campaigning noisily for his parole. An autobiographical novel, *Purgatory*, was even made into a movie. By 1990 the clamor had reached such a pitch that the authorities could no longer turn a deaf ear. On May 23, 1990, after serving 15 years, Jack Unterweger was released.

MEDIA DARLING

He slipped easily into the Vienna coffeehouse culture, where he was feted as a rising literary star. Television appearances followed, as did radio work and journalism, and it was the latter capacity that allowed him to cover the red-light murders in Vienna from an unusual perspective. Dressed in a distinctive white suit, Unterweger cut a languid figure on the talk show circuit. He spoke earnestly of his incarceration and how it had changed him. One thing he neglected to mention was that, just five months after his release, he had traveled to Graz, a city two hours southwest of Vienna by car, and murdered a prostitute named Brunhilde Masser and dumped her body in some woods. Six weeks later, on December 6, 1990, he returned to Graz and repeated the process with a young woman named Heidemarie Hammerer. Unterweger's next victim in Graz was Elfriede Schrempf, who he killed on March 8, 1991.

Then came a brief hiatus, shattered by his explosive four-murder spree that erupted in Vienna in the spring of 1991.

On June 10, 1991, Unterweger reappeared at Edelbacher's office, saying that he was bound for Los Angeles. He explained that he had been commissioned to write an article on crime and law enforcement in that city, and he wondered if Edelbacher had any contacts in the LAPD. Edelbacher, who by this time was deeply suspicious of Unterweger, said that he was unable to assist.

Undeterred, Unterweger headed for Los Angeles and checked into the Hotel Cecil on Seventh and Main, close to the downtown police department headquarters. Within days of his arrival, Shannon Exley was strangled. Less than three days after this, Unterweger called at the police headquarters, flashing his Austrian press credentials and seeking permission to ride with patrol officers. The force obliged and Unterweger got to see firsthand the city's seediest districts. During his brief stay in Los Angeles, Unterweger was unsuccessful in pitching a movie idea, but he did find time to throttle the life out of Irene Rodriguez and Sherri Long. Then he got on a plane and flew back to Austria.

While he had been away, the body of Sylvia Zagler had been discovered in the Vienna Woods. In addition, the Viennese police had received a tip-off. A retired detective living in Salzburg, August Schenner, disturbed by newspaper accounts of the murder spree, contacted officers working on the case. He told them of a 1973 murder he had investigated, involving a female Yugoslav factory worker, Marica Horvath, 23, who had been dragged from Lake Salzach. By the time he had amassed enough evidence to charge his prime suspect, the man was already serving a life sentence for murder, so he was ordered to drop the Horvath case. That suspect was Jack Unterweger.

This latest development put the spotlight on Unterweger. He responded with a string of articles, criticizing the police for their ineffectual efforts to capture the "Vienna Woods Killer." But the net around him was drawing tighter.

A few days later, a Teletype message arrived at Vienna's police headquarters. Inspectors in Graz investigating the recent murders of Brunhilde Masser and Heidemarie Hammerer had made the connection to the Vienna killings, and they had a lead. A young prostitute had come to them, they said, and told how a man driving a white Ford Mustang convertible had picked her up and driven her out to some woods, paid her, then handcuffed her. When she became frightened and started to

Interpol employees work in the control room of Operation Infra-Red in Lyon, France, in July 2010. The operation was aimed at tracking down 450 particularly dangerous fugitives. (*AP Photo/Laurent Cipriani*)

cry, he inexplicably released her. From the personalized license plate on the car—JACK 1—police had no difficulty in tracing the driver. When shown a photograph of Unterweger, she unhesitatingly identified him as her attacker.

Unterweger now became the focus of a huge surveillance operation, with every aspect of his life under scrutiny. Credit card bills placed him in Graz and Vienna at the times of the murders. Attempts were made to trace his cars—he had owned six in two years—but each had been methodically cleaned and offered no evidentiary assistance.

By this time the Austrian press had the scent of blood in their nostrils. Overnight, Unterweger, the "media darling," became Unterweger, the "media monster," as frenzied reports prematurely announced that a warrant had been issued for his arrest. Unterweger was not taking any chances. With his latest girlfriend, 18-year-old Bianca Mrak, at his side, he fled.

Interpol became involved at this juncture of the investigation. Agents tracked Unterweger through Switzerland and then on to France. On each leg of his journey, Unterweger, as narcissistic and self-serving as ever, took time out to call the Austrian press to protest his innocence. He also phoned the police in Graz with the same story, but by now the evidence against him was building. Geiger's detectives had raided Unterweger's Vienna apartment, where they found street maps of Los Angeles and a menu from a restaurant in Malibu. There were also photographs of Unterweger posing with female LAPD members. A spate of transatlantic phone calls established that, during his stay in Los Angeles from June 11 to July 16, 1991, Unterweger had stayed in hotels immediately adjacent to the areas where the three murdered prostitutes had last been seen alive.

When the FBI was asked to run the Austrian killings through VICAP, using six indicators—female, prostitute, aged 19 to 35, found nude or seminude, ligature strangled, body disposed of in remote, wooded area—it flagged four matches. One, an unrelated crime, had been solved, but the other three were the murders in Los Angeles, all committed while Jack Unterweger was in town.

Interpol, meanwhile, was still keeping tabs on Unterweger through his credit card receipts, and these revealed that Unterweger and Bianca had boarded a plane in Paris, bound for Miami. The U.S. authorities were told that Unterweger was believed to be holed up somewhere in Miami Beach. Interpol wired a photo of Unterweger, as well as a description—5 feet 6 inches, early 40s, with pale skin, and tattoos on his upper arms. On February 27, 1992, agents from the U.S. Marshals Service, acting on a lead from Interpol, were staking out a Miami Beach money transfer store when, as predicted, Unterweger sauntered up, looking every inch the suntanned tourist.

But his highly tuned self-preservation antennae were always on alert and suddenly they began to twitch. Without warning, he turned and ran off down an alley. After a brief chase, he was arrested and taken into custody, sobbing all the way.

Unterweger knew the game was up and immediately waived his right to fight extradition proceedings. Although he had been arrested for a civil offense—entering the United States after making a false declaration on his tourist visa—he realized that this was just a holding charge, and he was desperate to get back to Austria as soon as possible. If he was tried in his homeland, he faced life in prison with maybe the chance of parole; in California he was looking at a date with the gas chamber. This is not to say that there was much likelihood of him ever being convicted of the Los Angeles killings. Apart from the fact that he had been in town when all three killings occurred—along with approximately 3.8 million other people—there was not a scrap of direct evidence against him.

Someone bitterly aware of this was Detective Fred Miller of the LAPD. On March 5 he received a call from the Department of Justice, telling him that Interpol, via the Washington NCB, had circulated a report to the effect that U.S. marshals in Miami had arrested Unterweger. Although Miller flew to Miami and interviewed Unterweger several times, he made no headway, and was certainly no nearer to being able to bring a winnable case against the smirking prisoner.

Nor was it by any means certain that Unterweger would be found guilty in Austria. He still enjoyed the support of many powerful figures in the literary world, many of whom refused to accept that their efforts had led to nine women being strangled. And then there were the problems with evidence. Although some red fibers microscopically similar

FREED TO KILL AGAIN

Another convicted killer with literary talent was Jack Abbott. While imprisoned in Utah, Abbott sent samples of his writing to author Norman Mailer. These were published, and Abbott's book *In the Belly of the Beast* became an immediate best seller. Mailer petitioned Abbott's parole board for the latter's release, describing Abbott as "a powerful and important American writer,"[2] and offering him a job. The board reviewed Abbott's record. Since age 12 (he was now 35) Abbott had spent less than six months out of jail. Minor thefts had led to more serious bank robberies. In 1966 he received an extra 14-year jail term for stabbing a fellow prisoner to death.

Despite official misgivings, Abbott was paroled. He went to work for Mailer as a researcher but lacked the necessary discipline and quit. In July 1981 he and two female companions visited an all-night New York diner. He got into an argument with a waiter named Richard Adan over use of the staff lavatory. The two took their quarrel outside, where Abbott stabbed Adan in the heart, killing him almost instantly. He had been free for just six weeks. Police traced Abbott to a Louisiana oil field and brought him back to New York to face trial. On April 15, 1982, Abbott was sentenced to 15 years in prison for manslaughter. He later died while incarcerated.

As it would with the Unterweger case, the Abbott tragedy generated bewilderment at the kind of foolishness that confuses literary talent with intellectual honesty. Some even raised concerns that, in both instances, weight of celebrity opinion had counted for more than common sense.

to those from a scarf owned by Unterweger had been found on the body of Heidemarie Hammerer, no scientist in the world could state that they definitely came from his scarf. Apart from this, the evidence against him was purely circumstantial. Indeed, prosecutors in Vienna were so pessimistic about their chances of securing a conviction against the best-selling author that they stepped back and allowed investigators from Graz to take the lead. Here, the authorities were much more steely nerved and determined to nail a pitiless killer who had thumbed his nose at the Austrian justice system. What they needed was strong direct evidence that would unequivocally place Unterweger at just one murder crime scene. Find that single link, they reasoned, and all that circumstantial evidence would suddenly take on a fresh and heightened significance.

At this point, the Austrian police went back to Interpol with a special request—had there been any other killings similar to those in Austria and Los Angeles, anywhere in the world? Interpol scoured its records. No other organization has such global reach when it comes to collating international crime data. In a matter of days, Interpol was able to provide information on a murder that had occurred in Prague, Czechoslovakia, just four months after Unterweger had been released from prison.

On September 14, 1990, a young woman named Blanka Bockova had stormed out of a bar in Wenceslas Square after arguing with her boyfriend. At the same time, at the other end of the square, Unterweger just happened to be wishing a friend goodnight. Blanka was later seen talking to a man aged around 40, but the details were sketchy and no one could offer any further clues. The next day Blanka's strangled body, covered in leaves, was found in some woods adjacent to the Vitava River. Her gray stockings were knotted tightly around her neck.

MISSING MUSTANG

Oddly enough, the Ford Mustang that Unterweger drove on his Prague trip was the only car that detectives had failed to trace, raising hopes that this might provide a significant lead. Finding that car proved nightmarishly difficult, especially when it was learned that the vehicle had been disassembled for spare parts. But the searchers refused to quit. Eventually, after two years of painstaking effort, the car seats were traced to a Linz garage.

On the passenger seat was a single hair. It was sent to a lab in Bern, Switzerland, for DNA analysis. Because DNA from hair can be extracted only from the root—and they had only one hair—it made for some extraordinarily delicate testing. In the end it yielded just 9 billionths of a gram of human DNA.

Serial killer Jack Unterweger leaves federal court in Miami in February 1992. Unterweger was sentenced to life in prison without the possibility of parole in 1994. *(AP Photo/Bill Cooke)*

It was enough. PCR, or polymerase chain reaction, is a method by which a few fragments of DNA can be duplicated into millions in a couple of hours. After complex PCR sampling, scientists were able to state, with a certainty put at 1 in 2.1 million, that this hair had come from Blanka Bockova.

On April 20, 1994, Unterweger went on trial in Graz, charged with the murder of 11 women in three countries. The trial was lengthy by Austrian standards, with Unterweger grandstanding for the jury and press alike. All his manipulation skills were on display as he airily dismissed the DNA evidence: "I can't deal with this scientifically, not at all. I just don't get this DNA stuff."[3] But the truth was, the DNA got him. On June 28 Unterweger was convicted of nine murders and sentenced to life without parole. Suddenly all of the arrogance hissed from his body. He was crying like a baby as guards led him away.

His incarceration was brief. Less than 24 hours later, using a rope fashioned from a thin metal wire and the drawstring from his tracksuit pants, this international strangler hanged himself in his prison cell. He used the same distinctive knot he had so cruelly practiced on his victims.

Interpol has long been used to chasing murderers who flee justice, but in recent years the agency has had to deal with the growing menace of the international serial killer. The Washington-born Dr. Michael Swango is believed to have poisoned upward of 60 victims in a murderous odyssey that took him across America and Africa. In the 1970s Charles Sobhraj, from Vietnam, left a trail of bodies in Thailand, Nepal, India, and Malaysia before ending up in a Nepalese prison. A German, Gerd Wenzinger, committed 13 murders in his homeland in the 1990s before killing four more women in Brazil. In 2001 American sailor John Eric Armstrong plea-bargained his way to a life term for four murders committed in the Detroit area, though it is feared that there may be many more victims around the world, killed during Armstrong's time in the U.S. Navy. Authorities in Hong Kong, Thailand, and Singapore are investigating claims that Armstrong murdered in their jurisdictions.

Finding the evidence, especially in old cases, to convict these long-distance killers of all their crimes, is a difficult task. Without Interpol's unique resources, it would be virtually impossible.

Unmasking "Mr. Swirl"

At the end of the 19th century, the invention of the automobile opened up a whole new world of opportunities for the criminal. No longer did the professional lawbreaker have to restrict his activities to the neighborhood in which he lived; instead he was able to roam at will, without the need for reference to transport timetables. A bank robber could commit crimes anywhere up and down the eastern seaboard of the United States, for example, and be hundreds of miles away within a matter of days.

A century later, the invention of the Internet took the criminal's mobility to an entirely different level. High-speed data link lines have become the new Model T. And this time around, the criminal does not even have to leave home to ply his larcenous trade. He can be munching sandwiches at a computer in Brazil, for example, having hacked into the bank account of some unwitting Californian, and a few clicks of the mouse is all it takes. Money can vanish from America and seconds later it might be whistling through the Russian banking system, on its way to an investment trust somewhere in the Caribbean. From there it can move anywhere. No doubt about it, the Internet has completely changed the face of criminal activity; and this does not apply exclusively to crimes involving money.

There is an altogether more sinister and darker side to cybercrime—the sexual exploitation of children. At one time pedophiles were lone hunters. Any packs that did form were usually localized and very secretive. On the Internet, however, they have been able to band together, either through Web sites or chat rooms. The growth of video, digital cameras, and high speed DSL connections makes it easy for sexual predators to record their activities, download files, or share images online. For the predator the crime is fleeting; for the victim it might result in a lifetime of misery and psychological damage, and his or her sufferings hold the potential to be circulated indefinitely in cyberspace.

The producers of Internet child pornography fall into two main categories: organized crime groups, who turn it into a highly lucrative business, and those who are sexually attracted to young children. In 2007 Interpol began receiving reports about a Western male who was leaving a dreadful trail of human exploitation across Southeast Asia. Ordinarily, Interpol is ultra-discreet about disclosing sensitive material of this kind. But this was no ordinary case. The stakes were far too high, which is why Interpol took the unprecedented step of enlisting the assistance of the world's biggest police force—the general public.

In Germany in 2004 a police task force charged with hunting down pedophiles uncovered 200 online images of men abusing young boys. The victims appeared to range in age from six to 13. Seventy of the images showed the same man. Although his face had been electronically altered, other identifying physical characteristics left no doubt that it was the same person in each image. He had used a high-end photo editing software package that allowed him to distort his face by giving it a pronounced swirl effect, thus making him entirely unrecognizable. Because of this—and because no one had a clue to his identity—he was dubbed "Mr. Swirl."

The man in the photos was obviously proud of his achievements. He had loaded the images onto various pedophilic Web sites, smugly confident that he had outwitted the world's law enforcement agencies. But he was gravely mistaken.

Investigators at Interpol's Trafficking in Human Beings department, in conjunction with the Bundeskriminalamt (BKA), Germany's federal police agency, began analyzing where the images originated. All computers hooked up to the Web have an identifying address known as an Internet protocol (IP). This leaves "footprints" wherever a computer user accesses the Internet. Tracking down this particular IP address

A Swedish police officer assigned to Interpol's human trafficking unit works to identify "Mr. Swirl." *(AP Photo/Laurent Cipriani)*

told investigators that the images had been uploaded from a computer in Vancouver, Canada. Now it was time to see what the images themselves would reveal. Most digital cameras store information in what is known as the Exchangeable Image File Format (known as .exif). Besides recording aperture, exposure, and various other camera settings, .exif also stores the date when an image is taken. From this, investigators were able to deduce that some of the abuse had occurred on March 29, 2002. Now it was a question of enlarging and digitally enhancing the images. One of these showed a leaflet lying on a bedside table. Zooming in at high magnification revealed a name—the Dai Hoang Kim hotel in Ho Chi Minh City, Vietnam. This information was sent to Interpol, which relayed it to the Vietnamese police. They visited the hotel, and confirmed that it was indeed the location in the image. The staff was questioned and the guest lists were retrieved and checked against passport pictures, but no positive identification could be made.

CAUGHT IN THE CYBERNET

Because the Internet has no borders—images uploaded in one country can be viewed anywhere on the planet—it has made the task of tracking down the international child abuser a monumental task. This is why the role of Interpol is critical in fighting child exploitation. To combat this menace, in 2001 it created the Interpol Child Abuse Image Database (ICAID). Containing hundreds of thousands of images that have been submitted by member countries, the ICAID is, first and foremost, a database designed to identify victims and locations. Image recognition software is used to isolate detail, to see if it matches any other images in the database. If a location is matched, and the country of origin identified, then the image is sent to police in that particular country.

Identifying victims and their nationalities and ascertaining when and where the images were taken is necessary for an international investigation to begin. As new images are received, they are entered into ICAID, adding to the base of information and increasing future chances of making an identification.

Thanks to ICAID, Interpol has been able to assist in the rescue of 535 victims of child abuse in 29 countries. Unfortunately, ICAID was available only at Interpol headquarters in Lyon, but as a direct result of successes such as Operation Vico, extra funding enabled Interpol to develop a new and more sophisticated system known as the International Child Sexual Exploitation database (ICSE). Unlike its predecessor, ICSE allows direct access for all member countries via Interpol's secure global police communications network. The most important advance is in the area of time-saving. Instead of making a request to Lyon and waiting for someone there to act on the request, information exchange is almost instantaneous, making it that much more difficult for the international sexual predator to evade justice.

LOCATION IDENTIFIED

Other images provided evidence of a second crime scene, with some shots appearing to show a particular harbor in Cambodia. Again, the local police confirmed the accuracy of the identification. Again, though, the trail went cold, as a check of local passport and immigration records failed to provide any leads. What these two geographical locations, Vietnam and Cambodia, did provide was the investigation's official code name—Operation Vico.

Still no closer to unmasking Mr. Swirl, computer experts at the BKA made a breakthrough. They had always known that the swirl effect in the photos was the result of the image being twisted in a clockwise direction. In all likelihood, this action had been performed by a filter. If

German specialists succeeded in producing identifiable images of Christopher Paul Neil from the original pictures in which his face had been digitally distorted. *(AP Photo/Interpol)*

they could find the same filter and reverse the process—twist the image counterclockwise—it was possible that an identifiable image might result. But there was frustration ahead. In order for this to work, the experts had to locate the exact center of the image and work from there. After much trial and error, eventually they found it. The image uncoiled to show a white male, with brown, receding hair, who looked to be in his 30s. In other images that the German experts worked on, the man was wearing spectacles.

Interpol immediately circulated these images to more than 50 specialized police departments in 20 different countries, but the answer that came back from all of them was the same—no identification. It was the same response when Interpol expanded the operation and sent the images to all of its NCBs. After two years of bitter frustration, in September 2006, Germany issued an Interpol Blue Notice. Once again it failed to uncover a name. Even ICAID, with its database of more than 520,000 child abuse images, was unable to offer any clues as to the man's identity.

Making the frustration doubly difficult to bear was the awful thought that, while the world's police forces floundered in Mr. Swirl's wake, he was free to pursue his vile attacks. How many more innocent victims, Interpol wondered, had fallen into his clutches since these images were taken?

It was this fear more than any other that eventually forced Interpol's hand. After long discussions in Lyon, on October 8, 2007, the organization did something it had never done in its long history—it requested assistance from the public. Images of the wanted man were released to the world's media and posted on the Interpol Web site, with the words, "Wanted: search for this man photographed sexually abusing children."[1]

Not everyone was happy with the decision. Anders Persson, who at that time oversaw ICAID, feared that releasing the images would let other pedophiles know that Interpol knew how to clarify distorted images, thus driving the perpetrators even deeper underground. There was also the specter of possible vigilantism to be considered, but the situation was too desperate, as Interpol Secretary-General Ronald K. Noble acknowledged. "For years images of this man sexually abusing children have been circulating," he told a press conference. "We have

RECENT EVENTS

In January 2008 two men checked in at Frankfurt Airport for a flight to New York City. The clerk examined their Canadian passports, issued boarding passes, and wished the two passengers a good flight. Eight hours after taking off, the plane touched down at John F. Kennedy International Airport in New York. As the two men passed through customs, a team of police officers swooped in and arrested them. While they had been in the air, their passport details were e-mailed to New York—standard procedure under Department of Homeland Security rules—to check against records of known criminals. This information was then automatically circulated to every available law enforcement agency. Four thousand miles away, in Lyon, Interpol's database of stolen passports flashed out a response—the passports had recently been stolen. It turned out that the men were not Canadian, as they claimed, but Sri Lankan.

This triumph was mainly due to one man. When Ronald K. Noble was elected secretary-general of Interpol in 2000, he became the first American, and the first non-European, to hold the post. As the former undersecretary for enforcement at the U.S. Treasury, he had been in charge of the Secret Service and the Bureau of Alcohol, Tobacco, Firearms, and Explosives. Such a strong background in law enforcement made him a good choice, but no one at Interpol had expected the new boss to make such radical changes.

Noble was mortified by what he considered to be the underutilization of Interpol's resources. Here was an organization sitting on a vast cache of data and information, and yet when he took over, Interpol was still sending out its red notices by regular mail. It was Noble's mission, as he saw it, to drag Interpol into the 21st century.

Just 10 months into his tenure, Noble, like billions around the world, sat in front of a TV screen and watched the horrors of 9/11 unfold. "That's when we knew the world had changed for Interpol," he said. "We went 24/7 that day."[4] Previously, Interpol had operated on regular office hours; now it monitored news and e-mails around the clock. And there was a conscious effort to shake off the apolitical torpor that had blighted the organization for so long. Any scrap of relevant information was fed into Interpol's ever-expanding arsenal of databases.

These databases have provided some stellar triumphs. For instance, 11 people carrying Cypriot passports were detained at Monterrey Airport in Mexico, after Interpol flagged the passports as part of a batch stolen in Cyprus. Careful screening revealed the people to be Iraqi citizens attempting to sneak into the United States to claim asylum (none had any terrorist connections). In May 2005 someone calling himself Michaël Tonia was arrested at the Canada–U.S. border crossing in Lewiston, New York, on suspicion of carrying a forged Canadian passport. When his fingerprints were fed into the Interpol database, it revealed that Tonia was really a Georgian named David Kricheli who, eight years previously, had been convicted in absentia of murder in Germany. He was extradited to serve his sentence. And then, in April 2007, DNA samples left at a jewelry heist in Dubai were matched by Interpol to two Serbian criminals who had escaped from a Liechtenstein prison in 2006. That same month, in a test of 1.9 million passport records collected over 16 days, U.S. border officials, using the Interpol data, discovered 273 stolen documents.

As a result of Noble's innovations, Interpol is now a more effective crime-fighting machine than it has ever been. The miracle is that it manages to do all this on a minuscule annual budget of $65 million, less than some sports stars earn in a year and roughly equivalent to what the New York Police Department spends in one week! Funding remains a constant problem. Noble continues to travel the world, banging the drum for Interpol, stressing the organization's unique place in global law enforcement. Today, more than ever, the world needs Interpol. Interpol may never have arrested a single criminal, but no one can doubt that, in its nine decades of existence, this remarkable organization has been responsible for putting an awful lot of bad guys behind bars.

tried all other means to identify and to bring him to justice but we are now convinced that without the public's help this sexual predator could continue to rape and sexually abuse young children."[2]

Once news of Interpol's historic decision hit the headlines, traffic at its Web site increased dramatically. And the tips came flooding in. Within a week of making the announcement, Interpol received more than 200 responses from around the world, all claiming to know the identity of the wanted man. Even Interpol was taken aback by the level of interest. "The public's response has been very positive," said Kristin Kvigne, assistant director of the Trafficking in Human Beings unit, adding that the department had also received "encouraging feedback from local and national law enforcement officers to our appeal."[3]

Most of the responses came in by e-mail. Eventually the total exceeded 350. Among the myriad "identifications," one name cropped up no fewer than five times. The first hit came inside 24 hours. Over the following days, identifications arrived independently of each other, from as far afield as Asia, the Americas, and Europe. Within just three days, Interpol had the suspect's name, nationality, date of birth, and passport number, as well as his previous and current places of employment.

THE CANADIAN TEACHER

Early in his life, Christopher Paul Neil, 32, had wanted to become a priest. He had studied for the clergy in his native Canada and had acted as a civilian chaplain at various sea cadet training camps in Saskatchewan. There his duties included offering spiritual advice for children 12 to 18 years old. He also worked as a substitute teacher. After a spell in a seminary in 2001, he was thought to have traveled to Southeast Asia, shortly before the image, date-stamped March 29, 2002, was taken. Once there, he was known to have obtained work as an English language teacher. His latest post, according to various informants, was at a school in Gwanju, South Korea.

Informants are not the only people who read newspapers. With his face plastered across the world's press, Neil panicked and ran. On October 11, 2007, just three days after Interpol's groundbreaking plea to the public, Neil bought a one-way ticket from Seoul to Thailand. Security cameras captured him that afternoon, arriving at Bangkok International

Airport. The image showed that he had shaved his head and was now wearing glasses. Passport and immigration checks confirmed that the passenger was Neil. Sadly, however, after such a promising start, the trail went cold again.

On October 15 Interpol announced that Neil was thought to be in Thailand, although the media report deliberately did not mention his name. The next break came when a 17-year-old Thai youth approached the Royal Thai Police with claims that Neil had molested him several years previously. This was sufficient for the local authorities to issue a warrant for Neil's arrest. Their lead was followed that same day by Interpol, which issued a Red Notice requesting Neil's immediate arrest, wherever in the world he might be found.

But Thai police were convinced he was still in the country, and, acting on information received, they began sifting through CCTV footage from hotels in Pattaya, a beach city notorious for catering to so-called sex tourists. Sure enough, on the day of his arrival in Thailand, Neil was caught on camera with a 25-year-old cross-dresser checking into a Pattaya hotel. Police inquiries in the transvestite community revealed the name of Neil's companion, Ohm; sources also provided his address and phone number. In addition, a trace was put on Ohm's cell phone. Piecing all this information together led the police to the city of Nakhon Ratchasima, approximately 150 miles north of Bangkok.

On the morning of October 19 police raided Neil's suspected hideout. When they burst in they found him unshaven and dressed in a grubby white T-shirt and tracksuit bottoms. He did not appear surprised by their arrival and said nothing, except to confirm his identity. The hunt for Mr. Swirl was over.

Interpol's jubilation was palpable. "That Neil is in Thai police custody just 10 days [sic] after Interpol's appeal to identify a man whose name, nationality and whereabouts were unknown is an outstanding achievement due to the co-operation between the police, the public and the media," said the head of Interpol's Bangkok liaison office, Colonel Panaspong Sirawongse.[5] It was undoubtedly one of the greatest triumphs in Interpol's history. Neil was a ruthless pedophile, eager to smooth the path for those with similar appetites. Internet bloggers claimed that Neil regularly posted methods for prospective teachers

Christopher Paul Neil arrives at the Thai Police Headquarters in Bangkok, Thailand, on October 19, 2007. *(AP Photo/Sakchai Lalit)*

from Canada to avoid police scrutiny when applying for teaching positions in Korea. They also stated that he fancied himself something of a computer expert, reportedly uploading instructions on how to wipe files from the Internet. As we have seen, Neil was not smart enough to cover his own footprints. Now that he was behind bars, it was up to the courts.

On August 15, 2008, Neil, who had pleaded guilty to abusing a young boy, was sentenced to 39 months in prison and ordered to pay his victim's family 60,000 Thai baht (approximately $1,800) in compensation. At a later trial, he was convicted on a second offense of child molestation, and given an additional six-year prison term.

Neil's incarceration will give him plenty of time to reflect on the great irony in this case: that it was the Internet that both tempted and caught him.

Chronology

1914	First International Criminal Police Congress held in Monaco; police officers, lawyers and magistrates from 14 countries meet to discuss arrest procedures, identification techniques, centralized international criminal records and extradition proceedings
1923	Creation of the International Criminal Police Commission (ICPC) with headquarters in Vienna, Austria, on the initiative of Dr. Johannes Schober, president of the Vienna Police
1925	The General Assembly, held in Berlin, proposes that each country establish a central point of contact within its police structure—the forerunner of the National Central Bureau (NCB)
1927	Resolution to establish NCBs adopted
1930	Specialized departments are established to deal with currency counterfeiting, criminal records, and passport forgery
1932	Following the death of Dr. Schober, new statutes are put in place creating the post of secretary general; the first was Austrian police commissioner Oskar Dressler
1935	Interpol international radio network launched
1938	The Nazis assume control after deposing Secretary-General Oskar Dressler; most countries stop participating and ICPC effectively ceases to exist as an international organization

1942	ICPC falls completely under German control and is relocated to Berlin.
1946	After the end of World War II, a new headquarters is set up in Paris, and "INTERPOL" is chosen as the organization's telegraphic address; Louis Ducloux becomes secretary general
1949	The United Nations grants Interpol consultative status as a nongovernmental organization
1951	Marcel Sicot becomes secretary general
1956	Following the adoption of a modernized constitution, the ICPC becomes the International Criminal Police Organization-INTERPOL, abbreviated to ICPO-INTERPOL or just INTERPOL; the organization becomes autonomous by collecting dues from member countries and relying on investments as the main means of support
1958	Contributions of member countries revised and financial regulations adopted
1963	First regional conference held, in Monrovia, Liberia. Jean Népote becomes secretary general
1965	The General Assembly sets out operating policies for NCBs
1972	Headquarters Agreement with France recognizes Interpol as an international organization
1978	André Bossard becomes secretary general
1982	An independent body is created to monitor the implementation of Interpol's internal rules in relation to data protection; this will become the Commission for the Control of Interpol Files in 2003
1985	Raymond Kendall becomes secretary-general
1989	Interpol moves its General Secretariat to Lyon, France
1990	The X.400 communication system is launched, enabling NCBs to send electronic messages to each other and to the General Secretariat directly

1992	An automated search facility for remote searches of Interpol databases is introduced
1997	Interpol's first Web site is launched
1998	Interpol Criminal Information System (ICIS) database is created
2000	Ronald K. Noble becomes secretary-general
2002	The I-24/7 Web-based communication system is launched, significantly improving NCBs' access to INTERPOL's databases and services; Canada is the first country to connect to the system; database of stolen and lost travel documents is launched
2003	Command and Co-ordination Centre is created at the General Secretariat, enabling the organization to operate 24 hours a day, seven days a week
2004	Interpol liaison office inaugurated at the United Nations in New York; first special representative appointed
2005	First INTERPOL–United Nations Special Notices issued for individuals subject to UN sanctions against Al-Qaeda and the Taliban
2008	Special representative appointed to the European Union in Brussels

Endnotes

Introduction

1. Fenton Bresler, *Interpol* (London: Sinclair-Stevenson, 1992), 10.

Chapter 1

1. Tom Tullet, *Inside Interpol* (London: Muller, 1963), 17.
2. Fenton Bresler, *Interpol* (London; Sinclair-Stevenson, 1992), 44.

Chapter 2

1. Harry Gordon, *The Times of Our Lives* (Queensland, Australia: University of Queensland Press, 2003), 277.
2. "Arrest Spurs Yachtsman Death Probe," *Washington Post*, November 13, 1951.
3. Stephen Kinzer, "Tale of Nazi Horror Unfurls in Stuttgart Trial," *New York Times*, November 14, 1991.
4. Marc Fisher, "Ex-Nazi Gets Life Term," *Washington Post*, May 19, 1992.

Chapter 3

1. British National Archives, *MEPO 2/10971*.
2. "Dr. Savundra in Fierce TV Duel," *The Times* (London), February 3, 1967.
3. "Savundra Gets Eight Years," *The Times* (London), March 8, 1968.

Chapter 4

1. United Nations, *World Drug Report* (2007), 170.
2. United Nations, *World Drug Report* (2007), 26.
3. Fenton Bresler, *Interpol* (London: Sinclair-Stevenson, 1992), 238.
4. "U.S. Breaks Up Money Laundering Drug-Ring," *St. Louis Post-Dispatch*, February 23, 1989.
5. Fenton Bresler, *Interpol* (London: Sinclair-Stevenson, 1992), 238.
6. John J. Fialka, "How a Big Drug Cartel Laundered $1.2 Billion," *Wall Street Journal*, March 1, 1990.
7. "Drug Suspect Arrives in U.S. to Stand Trial," *St Louis Post-Dispatch*, December 10, 1989.
8. "505-Year Laundering Sentences," *The Washington Post*, August 22, 1991.

Chapter 5

1. Fenton Bresler, *Interpol* (London: Sinclair-Stevenson, 1992), 283.
2. David Henry, "Stock Scandal Lands Jet Setter in Paris Jail," *Newsday*, September 18, 1988.
3. "French Charge Six with Participating in Securities Fraud," *Wall Street Journal*, August 10, 1988.
4. "Silent Key to $575M Share Sale Fraud," *Sydney Morning Herald*, December 1, 1988.

Chapter 6

1. Friederike Blümelhuber, "The Role of the Criminal Profiler in the Case of Jack Unterweger," http://www.ktpi.at/zeitung_corpus.htm (Accessed October 31, 2009).

2. Michiko Kakutani, "The Strange Case of the Writer and the Criminal," *New York Times*, September 20, 1981.

3. Rick Atkinson, "Killer Prose: Vienna's Literati Championed the Convict-Turned-Writer. Then He Struck Again," *Washington* Post, August 3, 1994.

Chapter 7

1. James Macintyre, "Interpol in Appeal to Find Prolific Child Abuser," *The Independent*, October 9, 2007.

2. Ibid.

3. "INTERPOL and its 186 member countries following up on leads to identify man in child sex abuse photos," Interpol Media Release, October 9, 2007.

4. Vivienne Walt/Lyons, "Interpol Finds Its Calling," *Time* Magazine, http://www.time.com/time/magazine/article/0,9171,1714806-2,00.html (Accessed October 20, 2010).

5. Ibid, October 19, 2007.

Bibliography

Bannon, David Race. *Race Against Evil*. Far Hills, N.J.: New Horizon Press, 2003.

Fooner, Michael. *Inside Interpol*. New York: Coward, McCann, & Geoghehan, 1975.

Fooner, Michael. *Interpol: Issues in World Crime*. New York: Plenum House, 1989.

Forrest, A. J. *Interpol*. London: Wingate, 1955.

Garrison, Omar V. *The Secret World of Interpol*. New York: Ralston-Pilot, 1976.

Gunther, John. *Inside Interpol*. London: Hamish Hamilton, 1940.

Hyde, H. Montgomery. *United in Crime*. London: Quality Book Club, 1956.

Johnsen, Trevor Meldal. *The Interpol Connection*. New York: Dial Press, 1979.

Noble, Iris. *Interpol, International Crime Fighter*. New York: Harcourt, Brace, Jovanovich, 1975.

Soderman, Harry. *A Policeman's Lot*. New York: Funk & Wagnalls, 1954.

Symons, Julian. *Crime and Detection*. London: Panther Books, 1968.

Further Resources

Print

Anderson, Malcolm. *Policing the World.* New York: Clarendon Press, 1989. Thoughtful critique of Interpol that discusses the possibility of alternative forms of international policing.

Bagley, Bruce M., and William O. Walker. *Drug Trafficking in the Americas.* Miami: University of Miami, 1994. Comprehensive overview of the cocaine trade, covering ways in which the drug cartels export their merchandise from South America to the rest of the world.

Blashfield, Jean F. *Interpol.* Milwaukee: World Almanac Library, 2004. Aimed at younger readers, this provides a basic introduction to the function and operation of Interpol.

Bresler, Fenton. *Interpol.* New York: Penguin, 1993. Well-sourced account of Interpol's formation and history that does not seek to airbrush the organization's more dubious operations during World War II.

British National Archives: DPP 2/4321. British government papers that detail the fraudulent activities of Emil Savundra over more than a decade on three continents, ending with his failed appeal against conviction in London.

British National Archives: MEPO 2/10971. Recently released British government papers covering the collapse of Fire, Auto & Marine, an insurance company fraud that left thousands out of pocket.

Conell, J., and D. Sutherland. *Fraud: the Amazing Career of Dr. Savundra.* New York: Stein and Day, 1979. Exhaustive study of the rise and fall of convicted fraudster Emil Savundra.

Ehrenfeld, Rachel. *Evil Money.* New York: HarperBusiness, 1994. This source tracks the many (and often imaginative) ways that criminals launder drug money.

Fooner, Michael. *A Guide to Interpol.* Washington, D.C.: U.S. Department of Justice, 1985. National Institute of Justice report on the structure of Interpol.

Grosse, Robert E. *Drugs and Money.* Westport, Conn.: Praeger, 2001. Very accessible study of money laundering and how it has impacted the economies of countries in Latin America.

Henry, David. "Stock Scandal Lands Jet Setter in Paris Jail." *Newsday,* September 18, 1988. A journalist's in-depth coverage into the life and times of crooked stock-operator Thomas F. Quinn.

Leake, John. *Entering Hades: . . . The Double Life of a Serial Killer.* New York: Farrar, Straus and Giroux, 2007. Jack Unterweger was one of the most extraordinary killers in history. This book details almost every known aspect of his bizarre life.

Lee, Peter G. *Interpol.* New York: Stein & Day, 1976. Provides general information on the history of Interpol.

McCrary, Gregg O. *The Unknown Darkness: Profiling the Predators Among Us.* New York: HarperTorch, 2004. Written by the former head of the FBI's Behavioral Science Unity, this book strips away many of the myths surrounding offender profiling and shows how it is used as a tool in the struggle to trap serial killers.

Mickleburgh, Rod. "Wanted Pedophile Taught at Catholic Schools in B.C." *The Globe and Mail* (Canada), October 17, 2007. A journalist delves into the background of convicted pedophile Christopher Neil.

Naim, Moises. *Illicit: How Smugglers, Traffickers, and Copycats Are Hijacking the Global Economy.* New York: Anchor, 2006. Demonstrates how money laundering has become one of the great growth industries of recent years and theorizes that this is a direct result of changes in the geopolitical landscape.

Tullet, Tom. *Inside Interpol.* London: Muller, 1963. One of the first books to cover the development of Interpol.

Weiss, Gary. "The Mob on Wall Street: Why You Can't See It." *BusinessWeek*, March 24, 1997. An inquiry by *BusinessWeek* magazine into how certain sectors of organized crime managed to infiltrate legitimate companies on Wall Street. Especially strong on stock market scams.

Online

Crime and Investigation Network: "Jack Unterweger: Poet of Death"
http://www.crimeandinvestigation.co.uk/crime-files/jack-unterweger-poet-of-death/biography.html
Detailed biography of serial killer Jack Unterweger.

Interpol
http://www.interpol.int
Official Web site of Interpol.

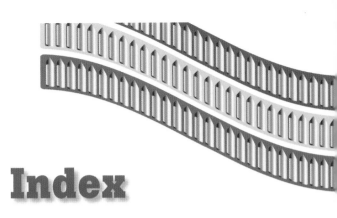

Index

About the Author

Colin Evans is a writer specializing in criminal investigations and forensics. He has written numerous articles and books, including *Blood on the Table: The Greatest Cases of New York City's Office of the Chief Medical Examiner, The Casebook of Forensic Detection,* and for Chelsea House, *Crime Scene Investigation, Evidence,* and *Trials and the Courts.* He has been a major contributor to *Courtroom Drama; Great World Trials;* and *Great American Trials.* Evans lives in the United Kingdom.